38256/70

D1313342

# GOD'S FREEDOM FIGHTERS

# GOD'S
# FREEDOM
# FIGHTERS

David C. K. Watson

Movement Books
Croydon, England

© David C. K. Watson
Minister at St. Cuthbert's Church, York
All rights reserved
1972
Fourth printing 1977

903221 00 4

Published by Movement Books,
A Division of The New Mildmay Press.
Movement for World Evangelization
10 Cuthbert Road, Croydon CRO 3RB
and printed by Coloprint, Hutton, Weston-super-Mare
Distributed on behalf of
Movement Books by S.T.L. P.O. Box 48,
Bromley, Kent.

To Anne, my fellow-freedom-fighter !

# ACKNOWLEDGEMENTS

The author acknowledges gratefully much guidance from Dr. Martyn Lloyd-Jones, who, in Westminster Chapel from 1960 to 1962, preached on 'The Christian Warfare'. Some of the material in this book was stimulated by those sermons.

He also is very grateful to the staff of The Movement for World Evangelization for their help in preparing the manuscript. In particular, he is grateful to Mr. John Fear, the Director of Administration of M.W.E., for all his encouragement and guidance. He is grateful as well to Miss Frances Smith in her careful reading of the manuscript.

He also wishes to thank members of St. Cuthbert's Church, York, for their fellowship, love and prayer in many of the spiritual battles of the last few years.

The author and publisher gratefully acknowledge the permission granted for the use of quotations from copyrighted material.

All scripture quotations, unless
indicated otherwise, are from the
Revised Standard Version of the Bible
© 1946 and 1952 by the Division of
Christian Education of the National
Council of the Churches of Christ in
the U.S.A.

# Foreword

"I am so glad to know that the Bible Readings given by David Watson at Filey at the great Christian Holiday Crusade are to be made available in print. They were listened to with the closest and most rapt attention by the great congregation of over three thousand meeting each morning in the Gaiety Theatre. The Bible Readings on the Christian's Warfare were both Biblical and intensely practical and their application to the daily situation in which so many Christians find themselves will bring great encouragement and blessing to many. To have them in this more permanent form will be of immense value."

(Rev.) GEORGE B. DUNCAN,
Minister of St. George's-Tron
Church, Glasgow.

"The outstanding feature of these Bible Readings is their compelling relevance to the age in which we live. It is more than time that Christians realized that there is a war on and that if Satan's plans are to be thwarted we need to buckle on the whole armour of God. These stirring studies will appeal to young and old alike."

(Rev. Dr.) A. SKEVINGTON WOOD,
Cliff College, Derbyshire.

# CONTENTS

# CONTENTS

# Introduction

In Ephesians chapter 2, Paul writing to Christians says this,
*'And you he made alive, when you were dead through the tres-*
*passes and sins in which you once walked, following the course*
*of this world, following the prince of the power of the air, the spirit*
*that is now at work in the sons of disobedience. Among these*
*we all once lived in the passions of our flesh, following the*
*desires of body and mind, and so we were by nature children of*
*wrath, like the rest of mankind. But God, who is rich in mercy,*
*out of the great love with which he loved us, even when we*
*were dead through our trespasses, made us alive together with*
*Christ (by grace you have been saved), and raised us up with*
*him, and made us sit with him in the heavenly places in Christ*
*Jesus, that in the coming ages he might show the immeasurable*
*riches of his grace in kindness toward us in Christ Jesus'*
*(verses 1-7).*

I want to look carefully at the whole theme of Christian Warfare because three truths have increasingly impressed
themselves on my mind.

First, *the intense reality of this warfare.* Here Paul is reminding the Christians at Ephesus that before they became
Christians they 'were dead through trespasses and sins';
and, in verses 2 and 3, you will see that while they were
dead in trespasses and sins they were following three things.
They were (a) following the course of this world, (b) following the prince of the power of the air, (c) following the
desires of body and mind, or the passions of the flesh. In
other words, he said, you were following the world, the flesh
and the devil. 'But God', he goes on to say, 'who is rich in
mercy', has saved us and delivered us from the power of the
world, the flesh and the devil. Christ has wonderfully set us
free; but He has set us *free to fight.* Therefore, every single
Christian is a freedom-fighter engaged in Christian Warfare.
And in Chapter 6 of this tremendous Epistle he says in verse
12, 'For we are not contending against flesh and blood, but
against the principalities, against the powers, against the

world rulers of this present darkness, against the spiritual hosts of wickedness in heavenly places'. Indeed, during the detailed preparation of these Bible Studies we have seen, in our own family in particular, and in our church to some extent, just how real this warfare is; the devil does not like to be exposed.

The second reason for this theme is that, undoubtedly, there is a *marked increase of satanic activity* in this country today. For example, there is a tremendous rise in spiritism in all its many forms: ouija boards, séances, black magic, satanic worship and so on. Three years ago one report estimated that there were 2,500 practising witches in this country alone. We shall look at some of the reasons for this increased satanic activity later, but at least, because of its presence, we should all the more be equipped in this Christian Warfare.

Thirdly, I find that *many Christians are sadly ignorant*, or perhaps forgetful, about this warfare. In pastoral work I am at times almost overwhelmed by what I call Christian casualties. One meets all too often fine Christians who are very depressed, or defeated, or oppressed by some dark powers, or suddenly filled with doubts or resentment and are aware that they are in need of deliverance. A missionary leader in Thailand told me some years ago that about 50% of the missionaries in that land had recently been invalided out through breakdowns and illnesses; and he said, 'I believe it is because we are largely ignorant of this spiritual warfare'.

In 1968 Robert Peterson of the Overseas Missionary Fellowship wrote his book *Roaring Lion*; and in his preface he said that when he came to this country to speak of some of the demonic activities which he had found in Borneo, not only did people not understand what he was saying, but most of them dismissed the truth of his words like this: 'It is nothing but hallucination, fantastic dreams'. He comments, 'The Old Testament deals with demonic activity in many of its aspects. Christ regarded demonism as a stern reality. The writers of the Epistles spared not in their exposure of these evil forces. Today we see the foolish heart of man darkened by the ceaseless activity of this host of seducing spirits. Can we in all honesty, then, let the "hallucination" statement above go by without challenge? I think not!' And he adds 'My prayer is that this book will help the Christian to know a little better the "depths of Satan" and by knowing, to help him "fight the good fight of faith".' That is my prayer for these Bible Studies. I believe there are few subjects which are more important for us to tackle seriously than this, and maybe for that reason few subjects which seem to be so little understood.

DAVID C. K. WATSON
York, January 1972

# CHAPTER ONE

# 'ALL THAT GLITTERS'

'The world' appears many times in Scripture with various definitions and meanings, but we can summarise the main truths by looking at the world in four stages.

**Stage 1: The Creation of the World,** as in Genesis 1 & 2. 'In the beginning God created the heavens and the earth' and 'God saw everything that he had made, and behold, it was very good' (Genesis 1, 31). Therefore, any form of dualism, which puts matter and spirit opposed to one another, is a false doctrine. 'God saw *everything* that he had made, and behold, it was very good.' Let us remember, then, that the body is good, and all that God has made is good, because God Himself is good. Further, God's creation of the world was planned for God's special creation—Man. 'Then the Lord God formed man of dust from the ground, and breathed into his nostrils the breath of life; and man became a living being. And the Lord God planted a garden in Eden, in the east; and there he put the man whom he had formed. . . . The Lord God took the man and put him in the garden of Eden to till it and keep it. And the Lord God commanded the man, saying, "You may freely eat of every tree of the garden; but of the tree of the knowledge of good and evil you shall not eat, for in the day that you eat of it you shall die"' (Genesis 2. 7-8, 15-17).

Therefore, God's creation is for man's benefit and for man's enjoyment. Man himself must still live in complete dependence upon his Creator; and God planned man's dependence to be a beautiful relationship of love between the creature and his loving Creator God. However, 'love' by definition risks being rejected. That is part of the beauty and tragedy of love: if I love someone, I risk being rejected by that person. Therefore, we come to—

**Stage 2: The Corruption of the World,** through the fall of man. When man rebelled there were two tragic consequences. First, *man's sin brought a barrier between himself and God.* At the end of chapter 2 verse 17 God says 'In the day that you eat of it you shall die' Therefore, in the day that Adam and Eve ate of that fruit they died, not physically but spiritually: 'Therefore the Lord God sent him forth from the garden of Eden, to till the ground from which he was taken. He drove out the man; and at the east of the garden of Eden he placed the cherubim, and a flaming sword which turned every way, to guard the way to the tree of life' (Genesis 3. 23-24). Ever since that day, although man has a hunger for God, because God has made him with a spiritual appetite (and hunger for God is one of the most obvious marks of society today), he has no knowledge of God and no experience of the reality of God *until* he finds God through Jesus Christ.

The second consequence of the fall is that *man's world was brought under the control of Satan,* and God's kingdom of light became Satan's kingdom of darkness—full of evil, sin, suffering, sickness and so on. In Genesis 6 you see a terrible description of the fallen world: 'The Lord saw that the wickedness of man was great in the earth, and that every imagination of the thoughts of his heart was only evil contiinually. And the Lord was sorry that he had made man on the earth, and it grieved him to his heart' verses 5-6). Later John says 'The whole world is in the power of the evil one'. James says 'Friendship with the world is enmity with God'. Paul says 'Creation is in bondage to decay and it groans for its redemption'. Although we may not understand the precise mechanics, because man was given the dominion and authority over the world when man fell the world fell, when man came under the control of Satan the world came under the control of Satan: 'The whole world is in the power of the evil one'.

It is very important for us to understand this clearly. It is all too easy to think like this: that on the one hand you have the 'Christian Church' with all its blessings; and miles away you have the 'world', with its drugs and drinks and gambling and sex; and that in between you have the perfectly harmless 'no-man's-land', the perfectly ordinary life of working, eating, sleeping, loving. Now these things are not wrong in themselves, of course not; but these *belong* to the world which is controlled by Satan. '*The whole world* is in the power of the evil one', including, therefore, the world of education, the world of philosophy, the world of politics, the world of entertainment, the world of television, the world of radio, and the world of the press. *The whole world* is in the power of the evil one.

Of course we see this in the standards and values of the world that we come across every single day. Look at today's adverts: 'Love is Harrod's food hall, love is those never-happen-again moments, an empty scent bottle, staying at home, love is a diamond, a diamond is a gift of love!' Or again, 'Tan like a filmstar, eat like a gourmet, live like a lord in the South of France. A holiday in the French Riviera is an experience you owe your wife at least once a lifetime!' But Jesus asked, 'What shall it profit a man if he gains the whole world and loses his own soul?' The whole world is in the power of the evil one!

In Luke 17.26, 27 Jesus said 'As it was in the days of Noah, so will it be in the days of the Son of man. They ate, they drank, they married, they were given in marriage' — notice these things: Jesus does not say that they lusted, they fornicated, they gambled. No! 'They ate, they drank, they married, they were given in marriage' (perfectly ordinary things), 'until the day when Noah entered the ark, and the flood came and destroyed them all'. Again in verse 28, 'Likewise as it was in the days of Lot — they ate, they drank, they bought, they sold, they planted, they built' (nothing wrong with any of these things), 'but on the day when Lot went out from Sodom fire and brimstone rained from heaven and destroyed them all'. Here Jesus mentions perfectly ordinary pursuits. Perhaps they did lust and fornicate as well: but here Jesus talks about natural, everyday activities. Why then did God's judgement fall? Because this was their whole world, this was their whole life!

Therefore, the problem for the Christian is not how to avoid buying and selling, eating and drinking, marrying and giving in marriage; of course not! The problem for the Christian is how to avoid the power *behind* these things. And there is only one answer that I understand from Scripture: that I must handle these things, even these everyday things, for the glory of God alone. 'Whether you eat or drink', says Paul, 'or whatever you do, do all to the glory of God'. Why? Because the *whole world* is in the power of the evil one. Even these ordinary, harmless, everyday things belong to the world which is in the control of Satan. Therefore, they belong either to God, if we can do them to His glory, or to Satan. Remember that when Jesus gave the parable of the sower, He described the seed that fell among thorns like this, 'They are those who hear, but as they go on their way they are choked by the cares and riches and pleasures of life' — ordinary everyday things, but things used by Satan to spoil God's work. 'The whole world is in the power of the evil one.' Oh, says someone, I must have that dress! (or that record or that car) I must have it! Must you? Have you prayed about it? Are you buying this thing for God's glory? Well, you may say, surely you don't pray about these things? Indeed we should, because when we are handling the things of the world we may well be touching the power that controls the world. Therefore, even with these most ordinary things we need to take them and use them for God's glory.

The Scriptures, as always, have a most beautiful balance:

far from being negative about the world, Paul writes in 1. Timothy 4. 1-3. 'Now the Spirit expressly says that in later times some will depart from the faith by giving heed to deceitful spirits and doctrines of demons, through the pretensions of liars whose consciences are seared, who forbid marriage and enjoin abstinence from foods which God created to be received with thanksgiving by those who believe and know the truth.' In other words, an excessive negative attitude to the world (you mustn't do these things, you mustn't do those things) could be a doctrine of demons! And he goes on (verses 4 & 5), 'For everything created by God is good, and nothing is to be rejected if' (N.B.) 'it is received with thanksgiving; for then it is consecrated by the word of God and prayer.' If we live our daily ordinary life for the glory of God, if we pray about what we do, if we receive these gifts with thanksgiving, *then* it is consecrated by the word of God and prayer, and it is good and beautiful and wholesome in the sight of God.

Now, bearing in mind that the whole world is under the control of Satan, two facts follow.

First, *The world refuses to know God*. (a) It rejects God's Son: 'He was in the world, and the world was made through Him, yet the world knew Him not'; and (b) the world also rejects God's Spirit, determined to exist independently of God. That is what we constantly experience even in Christian activities. That is what the devil is always trying to make us do: to act independently of God's Spirit in such a way that we do not acknowledge and glorify God's Son.

In a very important passage about the world, Paul writes to the Corinthian Christians, 'Where is the wise man? Where is the scribe? Where is the debater of this age? Has not God made foolish the wisdom of the world? For since, in the wisdom of God, the world did not know God through wisdom, it pleased God through the folly of what we preach to save those who believe. For Jews demand signs and Greeks seek wisdom, but we preach Christ crucified, a stumbling block to Jews and folly to Gentiles, but to those who are called, both Jews and Greeks, Christ the power of God and the wisdom of God'. (1 Corinthians 1. 20-24). Here both Jew and Gentile prefer the wisdom and the power of the world to the wisdom and power of God. I want to look at this more carefully for a moment.

The Jew, you see, represents the religious man; and it's part of the deception of the world that it may offer us a form of religion whilst denying the power of it. In Colossians 2 Paul writes, 'If with Christ you died to the elemental spirits of the universe, why do you live as if you still belonged to the world? Why do you submit to regulations, "Do not handle, Do not taste, Do not touch" (referring to *things* which all perish as they are used), according to human precepts and doctrines? These have indeed an appearance of wisdom in promoting rigour of devotion and self-abasement and severity to the body, but they are of no value in checking the indulgence of the flesh' (verses 20-23). In other words, the world says something like this, 'If you want religion you can have religion.' So the world offers us legalism or asceticism or ritualism or organization — anything which may have the appearance of spiritual wisdom, but which in fact is quite useless and a counterfeit of the real thing.

Indeed, you could sketch a fairly accurate picture of the history of the Church like this: God gives a wonderful fresh breath of Holy Spirit life (at the Day of Pentecost and at various revivals of the Church down the centuries) and man comes along and says 'That is wonderful! Now let's set up a Church Preservation Society!' Therefore man begins to work out a new denomination, a new church, a new fellowship, a new structure, a new organization, new rules and regulations, new patterns of activities — and the Holy Spirit quietly makes His departure. Does then this great organization collapse over-night? Not a bit of it! It goes on year after year, maybe century after century: the world's tragic counterfeit of the real thing. That great prophet of the twentieth century, A. W. Tozer, has put it like this: 'The Church began in power, moved in power, and moved just as long as she had power. When she no longer had power she dug in for safety and sought to conserve her gains. But her blessings were like the manna; though they tried to keep it overnight it bred worms and stank. So we have had monasticism, scholasticism, institutionalism, and they have all been indicative of the same thing: absence of spiritual power.'[1]

When I moved to York in 1965 we came to one of the twelve 'redundant' churches in York. Now what could we do with an empty redundant Church? We decided to have, apart from the very simple structure of Sunday services, only one organization: one mid-week meeting for Bible Study and prayer and in the very early days there were about five people, I think, who started to come to this. Four years later we still had only this one organized meeting for Bible Study and for prayer; we had no Sunday School, no Youth Club, no Young Wives, no Mothers' Union, no Men's Group, none of the organizations which many churches have. And some of my colleagues were saying to me 'How can your church exist without a Mothers' Union? How can you possibly manage without a Young Wives Fellowship?' But we felt very strongly that we would not make any move at all in establishing organizations until the Spirit of God made it abundantly clear to us. We knew that 'unless the Lord builds the house, those who build it labour in vain'.

I am not for one moment suggesting that every church should scrap its organizations. But the danger is these organizations can easily exist and go on existing for their own sake; then they belong to the world because they have lost their real spiritual purposes and life. Watchman Nee, in his very helpful book called *Love not the World*, has said this, 'The Church depends for its very existence upon a ceaseless impartation of fresh life from God, and cannot survive one day without it'.[2] Therefore if a Church or Fellowship or Organization ceases to depend upon the Spirit of God for

1 *Paths to Power* (Marshall Morgan & Scott).
2 *Love not the World* (Victory Press).

constant fresh life, immediately it goes dead and becomes a part of the world: holding a form of religion — sound, good, evangelical perhaps — but denying the power of it. You can sadly find today some churches which are sound, but sound asleep, lacking the life and power of the Spirit which is so vital if we are going to live for God and if the kingdom of God is going to be advanced. In student missions I have found repeatedly that the main obstacle to personal faith in Christ is, without question, the established organized church! Over and over again I find this thrown at me, and I am not speaking of one particular denomination. But we have to confess that the church as a whole has offered people religion which is the world's counterfeit of the real thing.

We turn next to the Gentile. If the Jew represents the religious man, the Gentile represents the secular man, particularly the rationalist who leans and depends on his learning, philosophy and argument. And again this is the spirit of the world which rejects Jesus Christ the Wisdom of God. Paul says 'Jews demand signs and Greeks seek wisdom, but we preach Christ crucified, a stumbling block to Jews and folly to Gentiles'. Further he expands on this in 1 Corinthians 2: 'When I came to you, brethren, I did not come proclaiming to you the testimony of God in lofty words or wisdom. For I decided to know *nothing* among you except Jesus Christ and him crucified. And I was with you in weakness and in much fear and trembling; and my speech and my message were not in plausible words of wisdom, but in demonstration of the Spirit and power, that your faith might not rest in the wisdom of men, but in the power of God.' (verses 1-5).

Let me illustrate this. I have personally benefited enormously from the work of Francis Schaeffer, and I have a very considerable respect for God's work at L'Abri. What is the purpose of L'Abri? Edith Schaeffer explains it in her book[1]: 'to shew forth by demonstration in our life and work the existence of God'. She goes on to say what she means

1 *L'Abri* (Norfolk Press).

by this, 'We have set forth to live by prayer in these four
specific realms:

1. We make our financial and material needs known to
   God alone, in prayer, rather than sending out pleas
   for money . . .

2. We pray that God will bring the people of His choice
   to us, and keep all others away . . .

3. We pray that God will plan the work, and unfold His
   plan to us day by day . . .

4. We pray that God will send the workers of His choice
   to us, rather than pleading for workers in the usual
   channels.'

You see that it is God, God, God, God-centered not man-
organized; and that is no doubt why God seems undoubtedly
to be blessing that particular work. Here is a fellowship
which seeks to depend on God for its daily spiritual life.
But it is dangerously possible for some Christians to take
Schaeffer's learning and Schaeffer's philosophy and
Schaeffer's culture and Schaeffer's understanding without
Schaeffer's *prayer*; and *then* it becomes the world's counterfeit. Indeed it is exactly the opposite of what Paul says here
when he claims that he came to Corinth in 'demonstration
of the Spirit and power, that your faith might not rest
in the wisdom of men but in the power of God'. In one
university mission that I was leading, there was in one hall
of residence an 'ultra-Schaeffer' group. They were very
critical of the form of the mission, and very argumentative
in the coffee parties. In that hall there was no sign whatever of God's blessing. How could there be, when the attitude of the Christians was like that? It was a tragic illustration of the spirit of the world which all the time seeks
to make us work and live independently of God. This is in
no sense a criticism of Dr. Francis Schaeffer, but an example
of what happens when our trust is in man instead of God.
And I have been disturbed in recent years by a number
of evangelical conferences and organizations and commit-

tees where the emphasis is more on strategy than on prayer. But unless we pray we are wasting our time. When we work, *we* work; when we pray then God can work. It is so easy to imbibe the spirit of the world, either refusing to know God at all, or refusing to depend on Him for everything.

However, the world not only refuses to know God; *it requires the worship of man.* Because of this, in 1 John 2. 15-16 John warns his readers 'Do not love the world or the things in the world. If anyone loves the world, love for the Father is not in him. For all that is in the world, the lust of the flesh and the lust of the eyes and the pride of life, is not of the Father but is of the world'. That, of course, is a reference to the original temptation of man in Genesis 3. Almost exactly the same expressions are used there. Satan knew that if Adam and Eve could become a prey to the lust of the flesh and the lust of the eyes and the pride of life, desiring to be as God and to know as God knows, then man from that moment on would worship and serve Satan, and worship and love Satan's world. Thus in Romans you get the appalling picture of man in utter bondage to the world: 'They exchanged the truth about God for a lie and worshipped and served the creature rather than the Creator' (Romans 1.25).

Some travellers once came to a desert island and they found there many moon-worshippers. The travellers said, 'This is very strange. If you really want to worship something in the skies, why don't you worship the sun rather than the moon?' They were told 'Oh, it's very simple; you see, the sun shines only by day when it's light and we don't need it; but the moon shines by night when it's dark and we cannot see!' They failed to see, of course, that the light of the moon depends entirely on the sun. Poor ignorant people! Yet today most people worship the creature rather than the Creator. They ignore the Source of everything and worship the things themselves. It is not surprising, then, that man is left with no answers to the great questions of today. In the musical '*Hair*' there is one refrain which keeps on pleading, 'Tell me why, tell me why, tell me why, tell me why. Is there an answer? Tell me why'. Man today is lost. But that is the inevitable consequence of a world that refuses to know God and requires the worship of man. With Stage 2 then, 'The whole world is in the power of the evil one'.

## Stage 3. The Reconciliation of the World

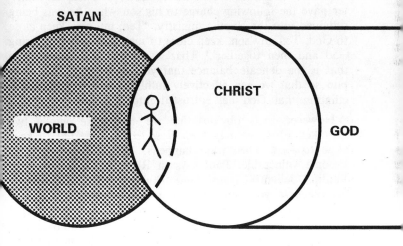

In 2 Corinthians 5, Paul speaking of the wonderful truth that 'if anyone is in Christ, he is a new creation', goes on to say: 'All this is from God, who through Christ reconciled us to himself and gave us the ministry of reconciliation; that is, God was in Christ reconciling the world to himself, not counting their trespasses against them, and entrusting to us the message of reconciliation. So we are ambassadors for Christ, God making his appeal through

us. We beseech you on behalf of Christ, be reconciled to God' (verses 18-20). As ambassadors our task is to bring the world back to God.

What is our place, then, as Christians? We are still in the world, yes; but we are *in Christ* in the world. In the diagram (page 25) the Christian's position is in that 'banana', which is created by the overlap of the two circles. We are in Christ in the world, and providing we abide in Christ we are not only safe from the pull of the world, but we are in a position to reconcile the world to God: 'We beseech you on behalf of Christ, be reconciled to God'. One Baptist minister gave the following charge to his son when he was being ordained into the Baptist ministry: 'Ted, my son, keep close to God. Ted, my son, keep close to man. Ted, my son, bring God and men together'.[1] That is a wonderful charge, and that is the delicate balance that you and I need to maintain so that we can effectively fulfil the ministry of reconciliation that God has entrusted into our hands.

However, it is obvious that we can make one of two mistakes. First, *we may keep close to man but fail to keep close to God*. Then what happens? Why, immediately we become vulnerable. Paul says in Romans 12. 2. (in J. B. Phillips' delightful translation) 'Don't let the world around you squeeze you into its own mould'—for this is a very mouldy mould as it leads us right away from the living God — 'but let God re-mould your minds from within'. How? 'By presenting your bodies every day as a living sacrifice'. In other words, we must daily abide in Jesus Christ; anything less than that could be fatal.

Here I want to be frank for a moment, at the risk of being misunderstood. For some time in evangelical circles we have talked about a 'worldly' Christian as one who smokes and drinks and dances and gambles and so on; and a 'non-worldly' spiritual Christian as one who doesn't smoke, and

[1] Quoted by Leighton Ford in *The Christian Persuader* (Hodder & Stoughton) p. 72 ff.

doesn't drink and doesn't dance and doesn't gamble. The point is this: these rules and principles, *by themselves*, are no protection from the world at all. I may never smoke, I may never drink, I may never dance, I may never gamble, and yet, in the New Testament sense, I could be a thoroughly worldly Christian! And that may surprise you. But the crucial question for me to ask is this, 'Is the emphasis of my life on *things*—doing things or even not doing things— or is my emphasis on Jesus Christ?' That is the crucial question. Remember that any legalistic attitude is the world's counterfeit of the real thing; and the real thing is a living, fresh, vital experience of Jesus Christ day by day.

Turning again to Colossians 2, Paul exhorts the Christians that 'as therefore you received Christ Jesus the Lord, so live in him, rooted and built up in him'. Therefore 'Why do you submit to regulations, "Do not handle, Do not taste, Do not touch" (referring to *things* which all perish as they are used)?' These things may have an appearance of spiritual wisdom but they are quite useless in themselves. Therefore, he says, 'If then you have been raised with Christ, seek the things that are above, where Christ is, seated at the right hand of God. Set your minds on things that are above, not on things that are on earth. For you have died, and your life is hid with Christ in God' (Colossians 2.6, 20-22; 3. 1-3).

Now you can see, I think, the strategy of Satan. You can see why many evangelical Christians or churches or fellowships have apparently gone dead even though they are still very careful indeed about what they do, or not do. You see, Satan says something like this: 'I see that most Christians in Christ do not smoke, they do not gamble, they do not dance' (so often we have a much better use for our time and money anyway). 'Therefore', he says, 'I will try and convince them that these *things* are the very essence of spirituality, and, provided they keep these rules they are safe'. Thus he lures us out of this position of abiding in Jesus, and we go to various meetings, and we don't do this and we don't do that and we don't do the other; but Satan has created a wordly Christian, because our pre-occupation is with *things* instead of with Jesus.

Let me illustrate this from something which happened quite recently. In our church, a young professional actress gave her life to Christ and was wonderfully born again. She came to see me a little time afterwards and said, 'Well, now I have found Christ do you think that I shall have to give up my acting?' I felt that, with this idea, Satan was tempting her to live by rules and regulations; so I said, 'No, don't give up your acting, but seek to deepen your relationship with Jesus and let Him guide you step by step'. All was well for a number of months; but suddenly she rang me up in great distress and she was crying at the other end of the 'phone. The one person who could 'make' her or 'break' her, the one person who was giving her jobs and who could do so in the future, wanted her to act in some play which, although not obscene, was still very light-hearted about sex relationships; and she felt, as a Christian, very unhappy about this play. 'But if I try to tell him that I cannot do it, he won't understand,' she said. 'He will be furious. What do I do?' And again I felt it was wrong for *me* to tell her. I said 'You go and talk to the Lord Jesus about it, and you let the peace of Christ be your guide as you pray about it. *He* will guide you, I won't tell you as I don't know. But He will guide you', and remembering this I said, quoting to her 1 Sam. 2. 30, ' " Those that honour me I will honour".'

A few days later she wrote to me this letter 'Dear David, I prayed about my work and God would not even let me *think* about doing that play. So I rang the director who, of course, was furious and could not understand, told me I was an amateur, that I should get out of the business, etc. etc. But while he was speaking'—notice this—'I felt so wonderful as if Jesus was smiling down upon me, a wonderful radiance difficult to describe.' And she went on, 'I have a great feeling of joy and am so glad to be able to do something for my God, and I will put my trust in Him for my work and for everything.' A few days later she heard that she had been offered a part in a film, a part that was exciting, glorifying to God and better in every way. God always honours those who honour Him; and the peace of Christ has ruled in her heart. 'He who abides in Me, the same will bring forth much fruit.'

The other mistake, as we try to live as Christians in the world, is that *we may keep too close to God, or rather the things of God, that we fail to keep close to man.* We may be so involved with Christian activities and Christian meetings that we lose any real contact with the world. Leighton Ford, in his book *The Christian Persuader,* said this, 'Part of Jesus' attractiveness, which drew secular people like a magnet, was His wonderful love of life, His natural, appealing friendliness. Luke shows Jesus going from dinner party to dinner party, teaching the Gospel to the guests. If Jesus came back today and mingled with gamblers, the skid-row crowd and the cocktail set, a lot of shocked Christians would throw up their hands and say He was too worldly![1]

Certainly it is not easy to keep this balance between really knowing God and loving Him day by day, and yet knowing man and man's needs and man's agonies and man's loneliness. Therefore Jesus, knowing all about the difficulties of this balance, prayed for His disciples like this: 'I have given them thy word; and the world has hated them because they are not of the world, even as I am not of the world. I do not pray that thou shouldst take them out of the world, but that thou shouldst keep them from the evil one. They are not of the world, even as I am not of the world. Sanctify them in the truth; they word is truth. As thou didst send me into the world, so I have sent them into the world. And for their sake I consecrate myself, that they also may be consecrated in truth. I do not pray for these only, but also for those who believe in me through their word' (John

[1] op. cit. p. 72.

17. 14-20). Here is the vital thing, that we should be *in* the world but not *of* the world. Just as a boat should be in the water but not the water in the boat, so a Christian should be in the world but not the world in the Christian. And for the sake of those for whom Christ died and who are going to believe on Him through our word, we should sanctify ourselves, and maintain this position of abiding in Him. There is no other place of safety and power.

On the whole we probably will not want certain 'worldly amusements', we have found something infinitely better—the unsearchable riches of Christ. But if we really love Him, there may be occasions when we find ourselves in certain situations, certain places, with certain people, that might surprise some Christians.

However, if at times that is the case we must watch very carefully two things: 1. 'Take care lest this liberty of yours somehow become a stumbling block to the weak' (1 Corinthians 8.9.)

2. 'Let any one who thinks that he stands take heed lest he fall' (1. Corinthians 10.12). An electrician may handle a 'live' wire; he knows what he is doing and he is quite safe, but he will be very careful indeed with what he does. So the Christian with the world.

Finally, and very briefly, we come to

**Stage 4: A New World Altogether,** when the kingdom of the world becomes the kingdom of our Lord and of His Christ. You see, this present world is temporary, it is passing away. And if I knew that a certain great firm was soon to be liquidated, I would certainly not put my money in that firm. I would expect no profit from that firm and I would not get involved with that firm. The world, too, is going to pass away. Why get too involved with it? As Paul says in Galatians 6.14 (J. B. Phillips' translation) 'God forbid that I should boast about anything or anybody except the cross

of our Lord Jesus Christ, which means'—notice this—'that
the world is a dead thing to me and I am a dead man to
the world!' I will not get involved and tied up with it because I find all my deepest needs met at the Cross of Christ.
There I find forgiveness, and peace, and love, and assurance,
and life—things that the world can never give. There God
Himself becomes real. And if you are still in doubt about
those 'questionables', these three practical principles have
helped me on many occasions:

1. Will it help or hinder my relationship with Jesus?
(Hebrews 12. 1-2.)

2. Will it help or hinder someone else's relationship with
   Jesus?

3. And, above all, is it to the glory of God?
(1. Corinthians 10.31—11.1.)

Plea:
Minds to consider.
Wills to control.

# CHAPTER TWO

# 'DYING TO BE FREE'

*'For those who live according to the flesh set their minds on the things of the flesh, but those who live according to the Spirit set their minds on the things of the Spirit. To set the mind on the flesh is death, but to set the mind on the Spirit is life and peace. For the mind that is set on the flesh is hostile to God; it does not submit to God's law, indeed it cannot; and those who are in the flesh cannot please God. But you are not in the flesh, you are in the Spirit, if the Spirit of God really dwells in you, Any one who does not have the Spirit of Christ does not belong to him'* (Romans 8. 5-9)

First of all, what is the meaning of 'the flesh'? Sometimes in the Scriptures it refers to physical existence; and in that sense, on at least three occasions in the New Testament, Jesus Christ Himself is described on earth as being 'in the flesh'. For example 1. John 4. 2, 'Every Spirit which confesses that Jesus Christ has come in the flesh is of God'.

However, in the above verses from Romans 8, the meaning of the word 'flesh' is very different. Here Paul says about Christians (verse 9), 'you are not in the flesh, you are in the Spirit'. Here the meaning of the word 'flesh' is not my physical body, but my self-life, my own natural and selfish inclinations, my earthly nature with all its natural lusts and desires. A very simple way of remembering what the word 'flesh' means is to spell it out, F L E S H, knock off the last letter H, turn it back to front—and there you have the word S E L F ! In Galations 5 verses 19-21 Paul describes 'the

works of the flesh' (Living Bible translation)[1]: 'when you
follow your own wrong inclinations your lives will produce
these evil results: impure thoughts, eagerness for lustful
pleasure, idolatry, spiritism, hatred and fighting, jealousy
and anger, constant effort to get the best for yourself, com-
plaints and criticisms, the feeling that everyone else is wrong
except those in your own little group . . envy, murder,
drunkenness, wild parties and all that sort of thing. Let
me tell you again, . . . that anyone living that sort of life
will not inherit the kingdom of God.'

*OVER*

In his book *The Spirit of the Living God*, Dr. Leon
Morris gives an illustration of the flesh in terms of a young
married couple going through a time of tragedy. The wife
was about to leave her husband, and at the husband's re-
quest the local minister went round to see her. He tried to
persuade her to stay with her husband and she answered like
this, 'Nothing that you can say will shake my determination.
I no longer love my husband. Life with him would be inex-
pressibly dreary. I have a right to be happy, and I mean to
claim this right'. Dr. Morris comments 'Those words, "I
have a right to be happy", perfectly express the mind of the
flesh. No matter at what cost to others, no matter at what
ultimate cost to himself, the fleshly person claims the right
to be happy. All other considerations must be subordinate
to that'.[2] That is the flesh.

Let us look again briefly at those verses in Roman 8. We
may notice five things about the flesh.

First, the flesh has weakened the law (verse 3): 'For God
has done what the law, weakened by the flesh, could not do.'
In other words, because of our self-life, the law of God, although good and right and perfect, cannot make man right
with God and cannot help man to overcome sin. We try to
keep the law, we cannot do it—because of the flesh.

Second, the flesh is sinful and condemned (verse 3) 'God

1 Coverdale House Publishers Ltd.
2 op. cit. p. 83 (Inter-Varsity Press).

... sending His own Son in the likeness of sinful flesh and for sin, he condemned sin in the flesh.'

Third, the flesh leads to death (verses 5 and 6): 'For those who live according to the flesh set their minds on the things of the flesh, but those who live according to the Spirit set their minds on the things of the Spirit. To set the mind on the flesh is death'. Therefore the flesh will profit you nothing, even if you feel you have the 'right to be happy'. It will always lead you to spiritual death.

Fourth, the flesh is hostile to God (verse 7) 'The mind that is set on the flesh is hostile to God: it does not submit to God's law, indeed it cannot'.

Fifth, the flesh cannot please God (verse 8): 'And those who are in the flesh cannot please God'.

Therefore, this self-life of ours would seem to present a most tremendous problem for every Christian, 'But', says Paul, with great emphasis in verse 9, 'you are *not* in the flesh, you are in the Spirit, if the Spirit of God really dwells in you.' And concerning our present position in Christ, and concerning our present freedom in Christ, I personally find no clearer teaching anywhere in the New Testament than that in Romans 6.

May we therefore turn to that chapter and concentrate especially on the first eleven verses. I believe it to be one of the greatest chapters in the whole of the Bible, and one which thousands of Christians throughout the world claim has made the most profound difference to their lives. Like all spiritual truths, of course, we need to be taught by the Holy Spirit. You may understand mentally and intellectually what this passage is saying, without really seeing it spiritually. I gave Bible Readings on Romans 6 for a whole year before I began to see the spiritual truth in my own Bible Readings! Looking back on my notes I see that it was all there, but spiritually I had not seen it. Therefore I would suggest, before you read any further, that you quietly ask the Holy Spirit to help you, to teach you, to speak to you, to encourage you, according to your personal need. The Holy Spirit is the Teacher of God's Word. When I came to 'see' what I had been preaching for some time, I found myself rather like that glorious Anglican clergyman of another generation, William Haslam, who was converted in his own pulpit by his own sermon! As he was preaching, suddenly he 'saw it', and someone at the back of the congregation stood up and shouted out, 'The parson's converted! The parson's converted!' And they all stood up and started praising God that the parson was converted! Oh for a good many more William Haslam's today! So do pray for spiritual understanding.

Now it is important to say at this stage that there is some division of opinion as to the exact interpretation of this passage. Paul is talking here about freedom from sin — all would agree with that. Some would say, though, that he is really speaking about freedom from the penalty of sin; others, freedom from the power of sin. In my study I have 22 commentaries on Romans; I enjoy them and turn to most of them, if not all of them, from time to time. Yet on this particular point of interpretation you can more or less divide the 22 illustrious commentators into two equal football teams; and it would be quite wrong and presumptuous of me to claim to be the referee and say which side is the winning side! These commentators are powerful names indeed, men well trained in the Scriptures. However, I personally find that the most convincing interpretation is the one held by such expositors as Dr. Martyn Lloyd-Jones, John Murray, John Calvin, C. J. Vaughan, Griffith Thomas, F. Godet, Nygren, and others—a very powerful team who I think are kicking the ball in the right direction!

First, we must look briefly at the chapters leading up to Romans 6. In chapters 1 to 3 Paul spells out the *fact* of sin, that Jews and Gentiles alike have sinned and are guilty before God and are under the judgement of God. At the end of Chapter 3 Paul asks how God can be both just and the justifier of the sinner at one and the same time. How can a sinner be forgiven and accepted by a holy God? There is only one answer: through faith in Jesus Christ and in His Blood. Then in chapter 4 Paul goes on to expand on the whole nature of the faith—the faith that saves. In chapter 5 we come to the apex of the whole book where Paul sets out the parallel and the contrast between Adam, on the one hand, and Christ on the other. Here are two fundamental realms in which everyone lives, and the diagram may help us to grasp this more clearly.

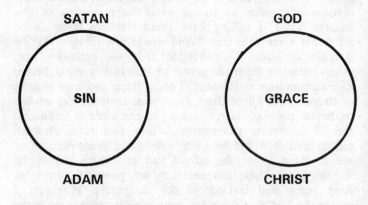

On the left there is the kingdom of Satan, consisting of all those who are in Adam; on the right the kingdom of God consisting of all those who are in Christ. In Adam we are under the penalty of sin, we are under the power of sin, we are bound by the law and subject to death; but in Christ we are set free from all things, and in chapters 5, 6, 7, and 8 Paul spells out the Christian's freedom. We are free from the penalty of sin (chapter 5) free from the power of sin (chapter 6), free from bondage to law (chapter 7), and free from death (chapter 8), meaning spiritual death. Paul is convinced that absolutely nothing can separate us from the love of God in Christ Jesus.

Now we can see how the opening question in chapter 6 fits in. In chapter 5 Paul has been explaining the complete and absolute forgiveness of sins in Christ. 'Therefore, since we are justified by faith, we have peace with God through our Lord Jesus Christ' (5. 1); and in verse 20, 'Law came in, to increase the trespass; but where sin increased, grace abounded all the more, so that, as sin reigned in death, grace also might reign through righteousness to eternal life through Jesus Christ our Lord.' Therefore in the diagram I have put SIN at the centre of the kingdom of Satan because sin reigns in that realm. In the kingdom of God I have put GRACE, because grace reigns in that realm. Now the natural question following those verses, especially 5. 20, is in Chapter 6 v. 1, 'What shall we say then? Are we to continue in sin that grace may abound?'

This chapter, then, has special value for two sorts of people. It is written first of all for a Christian who has such assurance of forgiveness that he may be tempted to be a little careless with his own life and behaviour. This can be a special snare in evangelical circles where we glory (rightly so) in the finished work of Christ on the Cross. Since I have put my trust in my Saviour I am forgiven and cleansed from all my sin. I know that if I confess my sin God is faithful and just to forgive me my sin . . . However if I glory in this without grasping the implications of this magnificent truth, it could be that I become lazy and undisciplined in my prayer and my Bible study. I might be apathetic when it comes to Christian service. I might become a little careless with my relationships, maybe with the opposite sex. I might become a little bit critical, a little bit unloving because I know that I am saved. I might become somewhat hearty or superficial or happy-go-lucky. I might forget God's holiness. I might forget the needs and problems of other people. I believe that many Christians, frankly, play with Christianity and flirt with sin. Well, Paul says here 'What shall we say then? Are we to continue in sin that grace may abound? By no means! How can we who died to sin still live in it?' If anyone has any understanding at all of the utter sinfulness of sin, that it ruins and spoils our lives; if any one knows anything of the holiness of God, who 'is of purer eyes than to behold evil and cannot look on iniquity'; if any one knows anything of the Cross of Jesus Christ—then sin *cannot* be a part of our lives. Someone has said this about sin, 'It can take the loveliest life in all the world and smash it on a cross'.

However, this passage is written also for the Christian who is depressed and defeated. He reads the great promises in the New Testament about victory over sin, that 'we are more than conquerors through Him who loved us'; and he sings with tremendous gusto that magnificent hymn of Charles Wesley, 'He breaks the power of cancelled sin, He sets the prisoner free'. But the Christian feels 'that's not true in my experience'. And sometimes there is a downward course: first of all there is a sense of *defeat;* and then there is *deceit* as we pretend to ourselves and to others that all is well, when in fact it is not; and if there is defeat followed by deceit there is very quickly *depression*, because 'it doesn't ring true in my experience'—and there are many depressed Christians today. Dr. Martyn Lloyd-Jones brought out his excellent book *Spiritual Depression*:[1] overnight it was a seller!

What then is the answer to these two very common problems: complacency on the one hand, depression on the other? From this passage two things are to be done: first, something for our minds to consider; second, something for our wills to control.

### Something for our minds to consider

The vital thing to grasp here is that Paul is talking about objective facts; he is not talking about subjective experience.

[1] op. cit. (Pickering & Inglis).

He is saying in effect, 'I'm not concerned about your experience; here are the facts of the matter which you ought to grasp'. Therefore he says, 'Do you not know' (v. 3), 'We know' (v. 6), 'We know' (v. 9), 'You also must consider' (v. 11). These are facts.

There was once a man who was quite convinced that he was dead. His friends tried to persuade him he was not dead, but that did not convince him. The psychiatrist also tried to persuade him that he was not dead but again with no success. Eventually the psychiatrist said, 'Well, I think there's one way I can convince him: I'll try to show him the fact that dead men do not bleed.' He showed him various medical text books, and eventually the poor man said, 'Yes, I see it! I believe it! I accept it as a fact; dead men do not bleed.' Whereupon the psychiatrist, with great presence of mind, picked up a little knife, plunged it into his arm, and blood flowed from the man's arm. He looked horrified at the sight. 'Goodness me!', he said, 'dead men bleed after all!' Here was a man *feeling* he was dead so that the facts made no impression on him at all. Now in this passage it is the other way round. Some people may *feel* they are very much alive to sin; but Paul is saying, 'No! This is a fact. You must know this, you must consider this; you are dead to sin and alive to God' (verse 11). I am told that the word 'consider' in the Greek was used in the realm of accountancy. It means that you have to make a very careful calculation. You must not make a mistake. You *are* dead to sin and alive to God.

Further, what Paul has to say here applies to every single Christian: 'Do you not know that *all* of us who have been baptized into Christ Jesus'—every single Christian, not just those who have special experiences but 'all of us'—'were baptized into his death' (verse 3). In other words, when Christ died on the Cross, not only did He die for us but we died in Him. And in the Greek this word 'died' is an aorist; it means 'once for all'; just as Christ died once for all, so we died in Christ once for all. Indeed you can see how insistent

Paul is about the fact of this death, because he stresses it in practically every verse of the first eleven verses. He is very emphatic.

There is a story of two sisters, Mary and Jane Brown, who were both converted the same day. The next day they were sent a formal invitation to some kind of party which they knew would be wild, and they felt, as newborn Christians, that they could not go to that party. Therefore they wrote their reply to the invitation: 'Mary and Jane Brown thank so and so for their kind invitation but regret that they are unable to come because they died yesterday'. That reply might not have been very good common sense, but it was very good theological sense; because now they were dead to sin and alive to God. Indeed you could translate verse 2 more accurately, to indicate the right emphasis: 'Shall we continue in sin that grace may abound? By no means! How can *we, we* who died to sin still live in it?' The emphasis is on the word 'we'. And once we realise what we are and what we have become in Christ, it is *unthinkable* that we should continue in sin, that grace may abound.

Let me raise two questions—A. *What does it mean to be 'dead to sin'?* There are various interpretations and I am going to mention very briefly the main ones, because many are confused at this point.

(i) Some say it means 'dead to the *influence* of sin', dead to the very desire of sin—the doctrine of Perfectionism. But that is manifestly false. See verse 12: Why does Paul say, 'Let not sin therefore reign'? If we are dead to the influence, why does he say in verse 13 'Do not yield your members'? John says 'If we say we have no sin, we deceive ourselves, and the truth is not in us' (1 John 1.8.) At one conference there was a speaker who was teaching some form of sinless perfection. The other speaker there was Charles Spurgeon, who was quiet and said nothing at the time. But the next day at breakfast time, I am told, he poured a jug of milk over the head of the speaker to test his doctrine. He found his doctrine was false!

(ii) Others say, 'This means we *ought* to be dead to sin'. However, Paul's words are not an exhortation; and if that interpretation is right why didn't Paul say that? I think we have to give Paul the credit for saying what he meant and meaning what he said.

(iii) Others interpret this to mean that we are *dying daily to sin*. Of course there is a great truth in that; but Paul here uses in fact this aorist tense throughout. He does not say that we *are* dying nor we *must* die, but we *are already* dead. We died once for all.

(iv) Many take this to mean that we are dead to the guilt of sin; and that is perfectly and wonderfully true. But I believe there is something even more than this here.

(v) This is the Gospel of Freedom from *all* the consequences of sin, including its power and bondage; and one day freedom from its very presence, when we are with the Lord for ever in heaven. Further Paul clearly has this idea of power and bondage very much in mind, for at the end of verse 6 of Romans 6 he says that 'we might no longer be *enslaved* to sin', and again in verse 14 'Sin will have no *dominion* over you, since you are not under law but under grace'. We must constantly keep in mind those two realms (see the diagram on page 42). Paul says in chapter 5 that in the realm of Adam, sin reigned. But the Christian has now died to the reign of sin from the moment of his justification. Now he has come out of that realm into that other realm; now he is the kingdom of God; now he is in Christ; now grace reigns in his life. Therefore now he is wonderfully free from this reign of sin. As Paul says in chapter 6, verse 7 'he who has died is freed from sin'; and in so far as we consider this as a fact and live in the light of it, then it will become true, increasingly true, in our own personal lives. Therefore we have already died, we are already free.

B. *How did we die to sin?* The answer, as we have seen already, is through the Cross of Jesus Christ: 'We know that our old self was crucified with him' (v. 6). 'If we have died with Christ, we believe that we shall also live with him' (v. 8). When Christ died and was buried, we died in him and were buried with Him.

Therefore I have put between those two realms, the Cross,

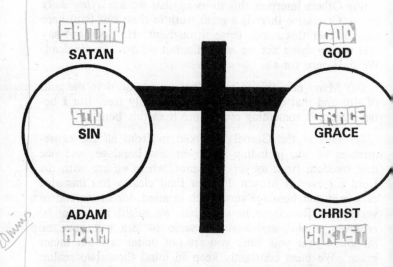

because that is the only possible way by which we can come out of the one realm into the other. Further, all that happened for us at the Cross was personally appropriated at the time of our baptism, or union with Christ: 'Do you not know that all of us who have been baptized into Christ Jesus were baptized into his death? We were buried therefore with him by baptism into death' (Romans 6 v 3, 4).

Now some people get side-tracked at this point, and as soon as they see this word 'baptism', they 'immerse' themselves in the whole question of water baptism, infant or otherwise, sprinkling or otherwise; and the devil loves to get us worked up on issues like this. Well, I'm not going to 'plunge' into this subject, not even 'dip' into it. Paul here is not talking about the outward rite and symbolism; what he is talking about is our union with Christ, as you can see so clearly in verse 5, 'For if we have been united with him in a death like his, we shall certainly be united with him in a resurrection like his'. In other words once we are united with Christ, we have already died with Him, we have already been buried with Him, we have already been raised with Him, and therefore *are now* dead unto sin and alive unto God. It is simply a fact, just as the Cross is a fact.

Let me try to illustrate this still further, as it is so important to see this clearly. Imagine a refugee escaping from East Berlin into West Berlin. In East Berlin he has known the fear and bondage and misery of that realm; but at last the moment comes when he is able to escape from that place and come into a different realm altogether, into West Berlin —a realm of freedom. Therefore he crosses that vital frontier, comes out of one realm into another realm, out of fear into freedom. From now onwards the authority that ruled over him in that old realm of East Berlin has no longer any legal right over him at all. They may shout at him over the wall, they may send him warnings and threats of all kinds. But now he is free, and no longer is he bound by their authority. Their authority has no reign or rule over him.

However, although it is simply a fact that he is now free, he may not immediately experience the full reality of that freedom. He may have nightmares, he may have sudden fears, he may still live as though he were in the old realm. But in so far as he considers himself dead to the old realm and alive to the new realm, then steadily and increasingly he will experience his freedom.

The parallel is obvious. God has wonderfully taken us out of the kingdom of darkness into the kingdom of light, from the power of Satan unto God; in so far as we understand our freedom in Christ, and believe it and act upon it, then indeed we shall experience our freedom; because in this realm of Christ, Satan has no right over us at all. Oh, he may shout at us and we may listen to him, and we may do what he wants. But there is no need to at all! Certainly the devil will try to make us doubt our position in Christ. He will say 'You think you are free, you think you are dead to sin and alive to God. But look at your experience! See how you're bound by your selfishness and your pride and your temper and your lust! You're not free at all—you're bound!' The devil is the father of lies. In his very first temptation he said to Eve, 'Has God said, . . . ?' Are you quite sure? Constantly he seeks to undermine our belief and conviction in the Word and promise of God. He will do the same here. He will say 'You are not free; you are not dead to sin, not at all! You are tremendously alive to it!' But we must hold on to God's Word. We must learn what it means to resist the devil when he attacks like this until he flees from us.

I remember the vicarage garden in my first parish. Sometimes small boys from the area would come in with their marauding forces to take some of the apples and pears from the trees. The vicar's son, aged then about 5, would stand in the garden with his hands on his hips and shout to this much bigger and tougher crowd, 'Get out of here, this is not your garden'. Well he had authority to say that! And we need to say to Satan, 'Get out of here, this is not your realm. I am no longer yours; I am a child of God. I am in Jesus Christ. Sin no longer reigns in my life, grace reigns. Get out!' And he will flee from you.

Although we are free, we are free to fight. We are God's freedom-fighters; but it is a fight of faith, and we need to put on the whole armour of God and take the sword of the Spirit to drive Satan away. Moreover, the faith that we need is wonderfully illustrated in Romans chapter 4 when Paul writes about the faith of Abraham: 'He did not weaken in faith when he considered his own body, which was as good as dead because he was about a hundred years old, or when he considered the barrenness of Sarah's womb. No distrust made him waver concerning the promise of God, but he grew strong in his faith as he gave glory to God, (or as he went on giving glory to God) fully convinced that God was able to do what He had promised. That is why his faith was "reckoned to him as righteousness" ' (Romans 4. 19-22). Now if Abraham had looked at his feelings and his experiences he would not have dared to believe God; but he looked steadfastly at the promise of God, and he went on giving glory to God. God's promise therefore became true in his experience. We need to learn to rest on God's promises.

In my first parish we had a glorious mission taken by that lovely Dutch Christian woman Corrie ten Boom — a wonderful child of God who has taught me personally so much. At the end of the week three of us who were the clergy in that church went down to the station to say goodbye to her. I think we were all wearing dark grey suits and white clerical collars — all very formal! Corrie got on to the train, and we were left on the crowded platform. As the train was beginning to pull out of the station, dear Corrie wanted to say something to us that we would remember. She therefore leant out of the window and shouted in a way everyone could hear, 'Don't wrestle, just nestle!' I think we all went a little pink! But I have never forgotten that: 'Don't wrestle, just nestle!' The struggle in the Christian life is not to struggle, but to rest in Jesus. There is indeed a fight, but it is a fight of faith, as we rest in the Lord.

Therefore, when Paul says here, 'We know that our old self was crucified with him so that the sinful body might be destroyed, and we might no longer be enslaved to sin' he is saying that the hold of sin over our bodies should have no effect whatever. He is saying, 'You *are* entirely delivered now from the rule and reign of sin. Don't be a slave to it, because you are not a slave to it. Don't live as though you were in Adam, because you are not in Adam'. A father may, perhaps, say to his teenage son, 'Don't be a baby!' He is not a baby, there's no question about that! But he is saying 'Don't be a baby; be your age, be what you are!' So it is with us in Christ; we must become what we are. We are in Christ, and sin shall not have dominion over us. Therefore we have this great word of exhortation, 'You also must consider yourselves dead to sin and alive to God in Christ Jesus'. Something for our minds to consider — a fact.

## Something for our wills to control

'Let not sin therefore reign in your mortal bodies, to make you obey their passions' (verse 12). Now, it would be ridiculous to say that to the non-Christian, for he is in Adam where sin does reign. He cannot help his bondage. But it makes a great deal of sense to say 'Let not' to a child of God; because now he is in Christ where sin does not reign. Paul, then, is saying 'Don't live as though you were in that old realm'. Therefore, when a Christian sins, he sins as a free man who is choosing to do wrong, or as a free man who does not as yet appreciate his freedom. Dr. Martyn Lloyd-Jones once put it in a striking way: he said this, 'The Christian who sins is a fool!'

You see, sin is a thoroughly wretched and miserable thing. From this chapter you will see, first of all in verse 16, that sin leads to *slavery;* 'Do you not know that if you yield yourselves to any one as obedient slaves, you are slaves of the one whom you obey, either of sin, which leads to death, or of obedience, which leads to righteousness?' Jesus once said, 'Whoever commits sin is the slave of sin'. Secondly, it leads to *shame:* 'But then what return did you get from the things of which you are now ashamed?' (verse 21). There is not a single Christian who can knowingly do something wrong in the sight of God and who is not afterwards ashamed of it. Thirdly, sin leads to *separation:* 'The end of those things is death' (verse 21) — 'death' meaning spiritual separation from God.

Therefore the Christian who sins is a miserable Christian. He has been robbed of the joy and peace that he ought to experience in Jesus Christ. Remember how King David, when he committed that double sin of murder and adultery, inwardly suffered absolute misery for a whole year, though outwardly all seemed well. You can see this in Psalm 32 which he wrote later after his initial confession of sin (Psalm 51). He now looks back on the situation, remembering that for a whole year he did not confess his sin. He says this, 'Blessed is he whose transgression is forgiven, whose sin is covered. Blessed is the man to whom the Lord imputes no iniquity, and in whose spirit there is no deceit. When I declared not my sin, my body wasted away through my groaning all day long. For day and night thy hand was heavy upon me; my strength was dried up as by the heat of summer . . . Many are the pangs of the wicked; but steadfast love surrounds him who trusts in the Lord.' I remember vividly a time when for some weeks and months I was seriously disobeying the Lord; and every time I went to church it was an agonising experience, because the preacher seemed to know all about me! And the Word of God went through me again and again. 'Many are the pangs of the wicked!' Indeed, whenever there is something in our life which is displeasing to God (and we know it) we are in a miserable and unhappy state. And because God loves us that misery and unhappiness will increase until we get right with God. Sin leads to slavery, shame and separation. Therefore why live in it? The Christian who sins is a fool!

More than that, he is despising what Christ has done for him on the Cross to bring him his freedom. Therefore Paul says in verse 13 again, 'Do not yield your members to sin as instruments of wickedness, but yield yourselves to God as men who have been brought from death to life, and your members to God as instruments of righteousness.' You are not in Satan's realm now, you are in God's realm through the Cross of Jesus Christ. Are you despising that? Dr. Martyn Lloyd-Jones once said that Christianity is far too often presented as a remedy for all our problems — 'Come to the clinic and we'll give you all the loving care and attention that you need to help you with your problems.' But, comments Dr. Lloyd-Jones, 'in the Bible I find a barracks, not a hospital. It is not a doctor you need but a Sergeant-Major. Here we are on the parade ground slouching about. A doctor is no good; it is discipline we need. We need to listen to the Sergeant-Major — "yield not to temptation but yield yourselves to God." This is the trouble with the Church today; there is too much of the hospital element; they have lost sight of the great battle.'[1] And if you are involved with a great battle there is only one thing that counts and that is your King and country. Your own personal needs and personal problems are unimportant. Everything must be for your King and country. So it is when we are engaged in this tremendous warfare, serving as soldiers of Jesus Christ. We need this element of discipline in the warfare. We are free indeed, but free to fight; therefore 'let not sin reign . . . Do not yield your members as instruments of wickedness.'

Let me ask you two personal questions which I have often asked myself. *Are you in any way acting a lie in your Christian life?* If you are a Christian, you are 'in Christ'; and if you are 'in Christ', 'you are dead to sin and alive to God'. But is any part of your life a lie to that? In your home, in your relationships, in your work, in your time and money — is any part a lie to what you are in Christ? If so, two serious consequences follow: first, you are denying the Gospel by your life. You are saying by your life 'Jesus does not save'. Krishna, having watched the lives of Christians for many years, had to say this, 'Christians claim that Jesus is their Saviour, but they show no more signs of being saved than anyone else'. And another Indian said this, 'I would become a Christian if I could see one'. Secondly, you are despising the Cross of Jesus Christ. Someone has said that

1 D. Martyn Lloyd-Jones *Spiritual Depression* (Pickering & Inglis)

sin is like slapping Christ in the face: 'You died for me upon the Cross, you bore my sins — but I don't care.' And the Bible has many warnings to the effect that if we continue in sin, having known Jesus Christ, we are crucifying the Son of God afresh and holding Him up for contempt. Are you acting a lie? Then you are denying the Gospel, and you are despising the Cross.

The second question is this, *Are you in any way defeated in your Christian life?* Is there some persistent temptation which always seems to hold the mastery over you? Then I pray very much that the Holy Spirit will help you to consider carefully your freedom in Christ — you are dead to sin, alive to God. I pray that the Holy Spirit will lead you to the Cross of Jesus Christ to confess that bondage to sin, to know His forgiveness and cleansing, and help you to claim the freedom which is yours in Christ. Christ has come to set you free, that you might not be enslaved to sin. Believe His Word, claim it, consider it, know it to be true, praise Him for it. And in so far as you believe it and act upon it, it will become true in your experience. Then you will begin to prove that Jesus saves, that Jesus sets us free. He does break the power of cancelled sin; He does set the prisoner free. That, I believe, is what the world is desperately waiting to see in our lives today.

# CHAPTER THREE

# 'THE RUTHLESS INVADER'

Why study the devil at all? Some Christians rightly point out the dangers of this: that Satan does not like being exposed. He is the great deceiver, and therefore to talk about him and to uncover some of his deceptions is rather like stirring up a hornet's nest. Why not leave well alone? Why not just concentrate upon Jesus? C. S. Lewis has warned us of a double danger: 'There are two equal and opposite errors into which our race can fall about the devils. One is to disbelieve in their existence. The other is to believe, and to feel an excessive and unhealthy interest in them. They themselves are equally pleased by both errors and hail a materialist or a magician with the same delight'.[1] However let me suggest four reasons why it is important to study the devil and all his works:

1. There are very many references in the Scriptures. Concerning occultism alone, with its dangers and consequences, there are at least 35 references. For your future study and reference see footnote[2] below.

2. We are not to be ignorant about these things. In 2 Corinthians 2.10 & 11 Paul explains the reason for some action:

[1] *Screwtape Letters* (Collins Publishers).
[2] Ex. 7. 11-12; 8. 7, 18; 22. 19; Lev. 19. 26, 31; 20. 6, 27; Deut. 18. 10-14; 1 Sam. 28; 2 Kings 17. 8, 17-18; 21. 1-6; 23. 24-25; 1 Chron. 10. 13-14; Is. 2. 6; 8. 19-20; 47. 9-15; Jer. 27. 9-10; 29. 8-14, 21-23; Ezek. 13. 17-23; Zech. 10. 2; Mal. 3. 5; Matt. 7. 13-23; 12. 22-28; 24. 24-25; Mark 1. 34; Luke 4. 40-41; 8. 26-33; 11. 24-26; Acts 8. 9; 16. 16; 19. 19; Gal. 5. 20; 2 Tim. 3. 8; Rev. 21. 8; 22. 15.

'To keep Satan from gaining the advantage over us; for we are not ignorant of his designs.' But many Christians today are.

3. We are to test the spirits. John says in 1. John 4. 1-3 'Beloved, do not believe every spirit, but test the spirits to see whether they are of God; for many false prophets have gone out into the world. By this you know the Spirit of God: every spirit which confesses that Jesus Christ has come in the flesh is of God, and every spirit which does not confess Jesus is not of God. This is the spirit of antichrist, of which you heard that it was coming, and now it is in the world already.' Now, how can you and I test the spirits, unless we know something about them and unless we know what this test means?

4. We are to wage war against the powers of darkness. Jesus said to the seventy in Luke 10, 'I have given you authority to tread on serpents and scorpions, and over all the power of the enemy'; and Paul in Ephesians 6 gives detailed instruction about this warfare, reminding us that 'we are not contending against flesh and blood, but against the principalities, against the powers, against the world rulers of this present darkness, against the spiritual hosts of wickedness in the heavenly places'. I believe, therefore, that we must study the devil and all his works, providing we start from the Bible and providing we are trusting personally in the Name and in the Blood of Jesus Christ.

## The Origin of Satan

We are not told very much except that Satan is a fallen angel thrown out of heaven because of the sin of pride.  (Isaiah 14. 12-14): 'How you are fallen from heaven, O Day Star, son of Dawn! How you are cut down to the ground, you who laid the nations low! You said in your heart, "I will ascend to heaven; above the stars of God I will set my throne on high; I will sit on the mount of assembly in the far north;

I will ascend above the heights of the clouds, I will make myself like the Most High."' Notice two things from that passage. First, Satan's name: he is called here 'O Day Star, son of Dawn', and therefore he is not a grotesque monster with horns and hooves and trident fork. Originally he was called, in Ezekiel 28, 'perfect in beauty', and can therefore well masquerade as an angel of light. Notice secondly, his ambition: 'I will make myself like the Most High'. This, of course, is reflected in his temptation of Adam and Eve, 'When you eat of this fruit', he said, 'you will be like God.' Anyway, because of pride and ambition Satan and his angels were condemned and thrown out of heaven; and the consequence of that fall is that Satan and his angels lost their heavenly bodies and are therefore now disembodied spirits, who, said Jesus in Luke chapter 11, 'are seeking rest'. That is why there is the phenomenon of demon possession. There one or more evil spirits will occupy a person (or maybe an animal or a house or some other place) because these spirits are seeking rest. Incidently, 'devil' possession should rightly be called demon possession; there is only one devil, but there are many demons.

## The Character of Satan

The word 'Satan' is the Hebrew word for adversary; and this is the most important fact about Satan. Peter calls him 'Your adversary the devil'. Notice that he is primarily the adversary of God, and not of people. The whole world lies in the arms of the evil one; and provided we are asleep in Satan's arms he is not particularly bothered with us, and we may not be bothered much by him: 'The strong man keeps his goods in peace.' You belong to his kingdom anyway; he will not give you a very happy time, for he is leading you to destruction, he is robbing you of the eternal riches of Jesus Christ, and his wages are death. But he is not primarily *your* adversary. But when you become a Christian and turn from darkness to light, from the power of Satan to God, then he is against you because he is against God's work:

and the more you are used by God, the more you are filled by His Spirit, the more Satan will attack you. This has been my constant experience—particularly when leading missions or engaged in directly evangelistic work. Often these attacks come on my own family.

Corrie ten Boom once said, when she began teaching Christians about spiritual warfare, "Whenever I gave this message, I was so tired I could hardly reach my bed. My heart beat irregularly and I felt ill'[1]; and she was tempted to leave this subject altogether and talk about something entirely different. Then she realised that Satan was trying to undermine her strength and her confidence in the Lord; she claimed the victory of the Name of Jesus, and found His peace.

Satan has many disguises.

1. *The vanishing trick.* In this Satan pretends he does not exist, and many people have been deceived by that. That is why the 'enlightened' churches of today which do not believe in the existence of Satan at all are often so lifeless and powerless. McNeile Dixon once wrote, 'The kindhearted humanitarians of the nineteenth century decided to improve on Christianity. The thought of Hell offended their susceptibilities. They closed it, and to their surprise the gates of Heaven closed also with a melancholy bang. The malignant countenance of Satan disturbed them. They dispensed with him and at the same time God took His departure.'[2] As the little verse puts it:

> 'The devil was fairly voted out,
> And of course the devil's gone;
> But simple folk would like to know
> Who carries his business on'.

2. *The Angel of Light.* In 2. Corinthians 11. 13-15 Paul writes about false teachers, 'Such men are false apostles, de-

[1] *Defeated Enemies,* page 11 (Christian Literature Crusade).
[2] Cited by F. J. Rae, *The Expository Times,* vol. lxvi, p. 215.

ceitful workmen, disguising themselves as apostles of Christ. And no wonder, for even Satan disguises himself as an angel of light. So it is not strange if his servants also disguise themselves as servants of righteousness. Their end will correspond to their deeds.' Satan may use certain messengers, who appear to be ministers of Christ, to teach new and intriguing interpretations of Scripture. Or they may claim some special and unusual revelation of God, going right beyond God's Word. Often they will show a subtle and mystical form of super-spirituality, as is particularly evident in the various sects. For example, Mary Baker Eddy wrote about her Christian Science textbook, *Science and Health*, these words: 'It was not myself, but the divine power of truth and love infinitely above me, which dictated *Science and Health*. I should blush to write this book, as I have, were it of human origin and I apart from God its author; but as I was only a scribe, echoing the harmonies of heaven in divine metaphysics, I cannot be supermodest in my estimation of the Christian Science textbook.'[1] To the unwary this may sound very modest, but it is of the utmost presumption to claim that her book has been inspired by God. And one further point to remember: the angel of light can easily quote scripture, and may do so freely.

3. *The Father of Lies*. Jesus says in John 8.43f, 'Why do you not understand what I say? It is because you cannot bear to hear my word. You are of your father the devil, and your will is to do your father's desires. He was a murderer from the beginning, and has nothing to do with the truth, because there is no truth in him. When he lies, he speaks according to his own nature, for he is a liar and the father of lies.' Strong meat! The great lie that he brings to us again and again is that he promises great rewards, as he did to Jesus in the wilderness temptation: 'To you', he said to Jesus, showing Him all the kingdoms of the world, 'I will give all this authority and their glory if you, then, will wor-

[1] *Christian Science Journal* of January, 1901.

ship me.' Today he may say to us, 'I'll give you an easy life; I'll give you success; I'll give you happiness; I'll give you riches; I'll give you wealth.' And Jesus says, 'What shall it profit a man to gain the whole world and forfeit his life?' This father of lies is a murderer from the beginning.

Again, he may tempt us to be super-spiritual, so that a Christian, for example, may refuse all medical help because 'the Lord is my doctor'. Now I believe that the Lord *is* my doctor, and I have no doubt we should look to the Lord more than we do for physical and mental needs as well as spiritual. But while it is true that the Lord can and does heal today, truth that is exaggerated becomes error. Heresy means, literally, going off at a tangent; so that within the balanced circle of truth that we have in the scriptures, if we take a point of truth and go off at a tangent, it becomes exaggerated and unbalanced. Then it is error. Satan knows all about those tangents. He is the father of lies.

Another common tactic of his is to spread false gossip and rumours about other Christians. This can do tremendous damage to God's work.

4. *The Serpent*, beguiling and enticing into sin. When it comes to God's Word it is very important that we stick to the truth, the whole truth and nothing but the truth. We must neither change it, nor subtract from it, nor add to it. In the temptation of Adam and Eve you will find that the serpent there does all those three things with God's Word, and therefore seeks to undermine God's Word. 'Did God say? Has God said? Are you really sure?' You see the same temptation at the start of Jesus' ministry when He was baptized. There God the Father said, 'You are My beloved Son'. The next moment Jesus was in the wilderness, and the tempter was saying to him twice, '*If* you are the Son of God ... *If* you are the Son of God.' He may likewise say to us, 'If you are a Christian, why do you behave like that? Why don't you feel more the reality of God? If Jesus is with you, why don't you know His power in your own experience? If

you are dead unto sin and alive unto God, why are you so selfish?' If, if, if . . ! The serpent.

5. *The Accuser*. John writes, in Revelation 12.10, 'The accuser of our brethren . . . who accuses them day and night.' The very word 'devil' means slanderer, and comes thirteen times in the New Testament. He may accuse us like this: 'You are such a failure; you are such a miserable Christian; look at all your sins. God doesn't love you, God çannot use you because you are such a failure!' Or again, Satan can accuse you by making you doubt if you are in the right place: 'You have mistaken God's guidance; you are in the wrong place, and where you are now God cannot use you!' And he gets you all bothered, wondering whether you have made some desperate mistake concerning guidance. Of course you and I may make mistakes about guidance; but as we surrender our possible mistakes to the Lord, He can take them and use them for His glory. But the devil goes on nagging, nagging, nagging. He is a tremendous 'nagger', trying to rob us of our peace in the Lord Jesus.

Notice his methods. Sometimes he creeps up behind us and whispers some blasphemous thought in our ear; then, before we realize what has happened, he whips round in front of us and says 'You call yourself a Christian! And you have got a thought like that in your mind!' In times of prayer have you known sometimes the most blasphemous, the most unclean, the most impure, the most lustful thoughts suddenly attacking you? Well, Satan, is the accuser; he puts those thoughts in our mind and then the next moment accuses us for ever having them there in the first place.

6. *The Roaring Lion*. This speaks of a particularly powerful attack, perhaps of fear, guilt, sickness, depression or possibly persecution. Peter, in 1 Peter 5. 8-9 tells his readers to 'be sober, be watchful. Your adversary the devil prowls around like a roaring lion, seeking some one to devour. Resist him, firm in your faith, knowing that the same experience

of suffering is required of your brotherhood throughout the world.'

7. *The Prince of the Power of the Air*, or the prince of this world; and as a prince he has a great legion of evil spirits working for him. In passing, the New Testament speaks of such spirits as the spirit of error, an unclean spirit (usually a spirit of lust), a seducing spirit (an overbalance of some truth), a deaf spirit, a dumb spirit, a spirit of fear, a lying spirit (giving false guidance or false prophecy), and a familiar spirit (manifesting itself through a medium). All these are utterly evil and opposed to God.

## The Work of Satan

Briefly, I want to look at Satan's work in three extremely important areas: *Cults, Schisms,* and *Occultism* — three vast areas, but it is important that we understand some basic principles.

## CULTS

By Cults I am referring, of course, not to other religions such as Buddhism, but to Christian Scientists, and Mormons, and Unitarians, and Jehovah's Witnesses and Christadelphians, the cult of Scientology, or Theosophy, or Spiritualism, and so on. The dictionary definition of a cult is this: 'It is a devotion to a particular person or thing as paid by a body of professed adherents'; and that is a good definition because nearly all the cults follow a particular person as well as a set of doctrines.

## Three main characteristics of the Cults

First, many of them seem, on the surface, like true Christianity. That is why, for some, they are so deceiving. I remember looking at some Mormon literature, and as I examined this beautifully designed glossy magazine I read page after page without discerning anything that was obviously wrong. It spoke about God, about Jesus, about the Spirit of God; it quoted the Bible — what was wrong with it? It was most deceptive.

Secondly, cults usually offer great blessings, sometimes far greater blessings than you will find in more orthodox branches of the church. The natural reaction of some people is, 'Why haven't we heard of this before? This is exactly what we need!' Often the cults flourish in times of stress and danger, perhaps a national crisis. Just after the last world war, spiritualism made great advances because of the many thousands who had been killed in the war. The cults offer special blessings for those who are sad or sick or anxious. At the moment they are having a field-day by concentrating on prophecies about the Last Days — a subject of growing interest because of the crisis in the world as a whole.

Thirdly, their adherents are nearly always sincere and zealous. They are quite clear as to what they believe and quite convinced of the truth of it. I have often asked Jehovah's Witnesses 'Why did you become a Jehovah's Witness?' So often the story is the same: 'I was longing to know God and I went along to my local minister. He was not able to help me. And at that time someone came and knocked on my door. He seemed to have all the answers and was so sure and so certain about what he believed that I listened and became convinced.' Not unnaturally the cults are enjoying some success today at a time when the established churches are discussing ad nauseam what they do *not* believe.

## Five objective tests of the Cults

1. The *origin* of the Cult. True Christianity depends entirely on the Person of Jesus Christ. Because Christ *was* and *is* the Son of God, what He said and did is of supreme importance. But with the cults, most of them are based on various leaders whose personal lives, by any standard, leave much to be desired. That is why Christ said

in the Sermon on the Mount, 'Beware of false prophets ... You will know them by their fruits.' Take, for example, Jehovah's Witnesses: the founder was a man called C. T. Russell, who was in several Law Courts for divorce and shady financial dealings. His successor was a man called Judge Rutherford; he was not a Judge, and was himself jailed for sedition.

2. The *Authority* of the Cult. Always you will find some special authority — for example, the Book of Mormon. And even if reference is made to the Bible, the main authority is always something other than the Bible; and it therefore undermines the supreme authority of the Bible. For example, the leader of Scientology, Ron L. Hubbard, says this, 'Thousands of philosophers have sought, every one of them from Socrates to Russell, the way to salvage the individual and society. All right we have found the way!' And if you are attracted by Scientology with its 'special knowledge', you need as basic equipment a Ron L. Hubbard Mark V Electrometer (which will cost you about £25), and then you have only just started!

3. The *Essential Doctrines* of the Cults. By these doctrines I mean, to begin with, the Person of Jesus Christ. This is the test of the spirit 'By this you know the Spirit of God: every spirit which confesses that Jesus Christ has come in the flesh is of God.' Without expounding this in detail, what John is saying here is that it is essential to believe that Jesus is both human and divine, perfect man and perfect God. Unless Jesus is both man and God there could be no Saviour, no Mediator between man and God. Therefore, in the Person of Jesus Christ, His Humanity and His divinity together are essential. But you will not find that to be so in the cults. They teach that Jesus was a great medium, or a great leader, or a great prophet, whatever it may be; but not both God and man. Or again, the doctrine of the Trinity: most cults are unitarian and speak of God in terms of 'the life force', 'the eternal consciousness', and so on; usually with little

reference to Jesus Christ. Or, look carefully at the whole concept of sin, and the atonement, and the need for repentance — almost always these are entirely missing. Positive Thinking says this, 'Believe in yourself, you're wonderful if only you realised it. The concept of sin is an insult; it is simply psychological.' Now, if you really believe that, there is no need of Christ, there is no need for the Cross, there is no need for Salvation, there is no need for the New Birth, there is no need for repentance; judgement goes, hell goes and, of course, with it goes heaven too.

4. The *Method* of the Cult. Usually there is a simple formula or technique for 'blessing'. I studied carefully a little time ago the Moral Re-Armament standard textbook called *Remaking Men*. There, there is no reference to Christ worth mentioning. I think His name is mentioned only once in quoting a verse of a hymn. There are just these four absolutes: Absolute honesty, purity, unselfishness and love. If you just follow these four absolutes, that is the secret of it all. There is always some formula, some technique, which replaces any living relationship with Jesus Christ.

5. These Cults are *man-centred*. A Scientology advertisement says, 'Free yourself from the barrier that holds *you* back in life, let the real *you* emerge' — God forbid! Dr. Martyn Lloyd-Jones comments on the man-centredness of the cults like this (the italics are mine), 'It always starts with *you*. It comes to *you* and tells *you* that it can do this that and the other for *you*. What do *you* need, what is *your* trouble, what is the matter with *you*? What are *you* looking for? Are *you* worried or troubled? Do *you* find it difficult to sleep? Do *you* find it difficult to forget *your* business or *your* profession? Are *you* over-anxious? Are *you* looking for peace? Are *you* looking for guidance?'[1] Christianity starts with God: 'In the beginning God', 'God so loved the World', — God, God, God, right at the very centre, right

[1] From a sermon on Counterfeits, preached in Westminster Chapel, 26th February, 1961.

from the very beginning. Not so with the cults.

## SCHISMS

*Schisms,* or divisions, and in particular divisions for inadequate reasons, were soon a problem in the early Church, notably in the Church at Corinth. Since those first days of the Church there have always been two main dangers for Christians: first, unity where there ought to be division; secondly, division when there ought to be unity.

*First, unity where there ought to be division.* I fear that the Ecumenical Movement has sometimes ignored this danger. Their favourite text is John 17.21, '. . . that they may all be one'; but a text without its context is a pretext. And the context of this verse is *unity based on truth.* In John 17. 17, 19 Jesus prayed 'Sanctify them in the truth; thy word is truth . . . And for their sake I consecrate myself, that they also may be consecrated in truth.'

Here Christ was praying first and foremost for His apostles who were already agreed about the essential truths and doctrines, and therefore He was praying that they might not divide over secondary matters. But if a person denies the divinity of Christ, the atonement, or justification by faith, or the resurrection of Christ, or the necessity of new birth, or the authority of Scripture — how can there be any true spiritual unity when there are basic differences over the very essentials of faith?

*Secondly, division where there ought to be unity.* You may know the parody of that famous hymn —

> 'Like a mighty tortoise moves the Church of God;
> Brothers we are treading where we've always trod.
> We are all divided, many bodies we;
> Very strong on doctrine, weak on charity.'

There are at least five matters where it is wrong for Christians to divide. First, it is wrong to divide over *personalities:* 'I belong to Paul, I belong to Cephas'. There is a tremendous cult of personality at the moment, with Christians flitting from church to church, from convention to convention — not because of the life and truth there, but because of their favourite personality. Secondly, it is wrong to divide on *positions of influence,* as did Diotrophes who liked to put himself first, or James and John who were asking for the places either side of Christ's throne in glory. Thirdly, it is wrong to divide over *social status,* paying attention to a rich man, 'Have a seat here, please' while saying to a poor man, 'Stand there', or 'Sit at my feet' (see James 2. 1-7). Fourthly, it is wrong to divide over *spiritual gifts;* you may have one gift, I may have another gift; but we should be neither jealous nor proud. We are members together of the one Body of Christ. Fifthly, it is wrong to divide on *minor doctrinal issues,* however important you and I may feel these doctrines to be. No one person has a complete monopoly of all aspects of God's truth. We all at the moment 'see in a mirror dimly'. There are certain vital issues that should bind together all those who know and love the Lord Jesus; but there are many other issues where I may personally believe something, but cannot really say I *know* I am right and that all others are wrong. That is a characteristic attitude of the flesh ('the feeling that everyone else is wrong except those in your own little group'). Take prophecy, for example: you may be a pre-millennialist, a post-millennialist, or an a-millennialist. Or you may not have the faintest clue what a millennialist is anyway! But how ridiculous to let the devil divide us on such matters as these! We need a certain amount of humility, and not bigotry, when it comes to these secondary matters.

## OCCULTISM

It may be helpful to follow the divisions suggested by Dr. Kurt Koch in his book *Occult Bondage and Deliverance.*[1]

[1] op. cit. (Hughes & Coleman).

First, there is *fortune-telling*, such as astrology, palmistry, clairvoyance and so on. According to one fairly recent opinion poll, more than two-thirds of Britain's adults read their horoscopes, and about one fifth, or seven million, take them seriously. Over one third of the adult population in this country believes in fortune telling. Sometimes, of course, it is all manifestly a fake: on the very first day of the postal strike in this country, when not a single letter was being delivered, one of the horoscopes in the daily papers said 'You will receive today a letter of considerable importance!' — which was a prophecy of a miracle indeed!

Nevertheless, there have been some brilliant predictions. Perhaps the most famous of all in recent years was on November 22nd, 1963, when a certain Jean Dixon said to her friends in Washington, 'My mind isn't at ease. I am afraid our President will suffer something terrible today.' Shortly after that, news was flashed throughout the whole world that President Kennedy had been assassinated. Jean Dixon has become perhaps the best known fortune teller in America, and this was not her first prediction; she has made a number of remarkable predictions and her books sell very widely.

Indeed, there is a very marked rise on astrology at the moment with books on almost any subject you can think of: 'Astrology made practical' — 'Astrology made easy' — 'Astrology for every day living' — 'Astrology guide to health and diet' — 'Astrology guide to your sex life' (some of the current titles).

Secondly, there is *magic*, black or white. Of course don't be deceived by those distinctions. All magic is black and satanic in the sight of God. By 'magic' I am referring to either the healing or the inflicting of diseases, charms and curses and the like. Examples of such magicians in the New Testament would be Simon Magus and Elymas the sorcerer. And this is very real today.

Let me give you just one story. One man felt called into the Church of England ministry and went to a theological college in this country. He was a married man with children and had been working in West Africa. During his time at college he was tremendously depressed, so depressed, even after psychiatric treatment, that the Principal of that college felt that he could not possibly be ordained. However, at the Principal's suggestion he went to see some Christian friends of mine. Together they prayed that God would reveal to one of them what was the basic cause of this depression; and it was in prayer that the man himself saw a vision. He saw that his African boy, who had been sacked for some theft, had gone along to the local witchdoctor and had a curse put upon him. Having seen this in the vision in prayer, the man came back to the small group of praying friends; and together they claimed the victory of Jesus and His blood. That man today is a normal, healthy, active minister of the Gospel of Jesus Christ.

Thirdly, there is *Spiritism*, with such things as table lifting, glass moving, speaking in a trance, automatic writing, and spiritualism (which is the religion of spiritism). In other words I am referring to spirit communication, or what the Bible calls necromancy. This is very common indeed, and there has recently been an enormous rise of this with ouija boards being sold in shops as party games. So common is spiritism today that in Paris, according to *Time* magazine, there is one priest for every 5,000 people, one doctor for every 514, one spiritualist for every 120.

Now what can be said about *Occultism* in general, in all of its many forms? First, it is *devilish*. One of the great passages on this is Deut. 18. 9-14. There God says, 'When you come into the land which the Lord your God gives you, you shall not learn to follow the abominable practices of those nations. There shall not be found among you any one who burns his son or his daughter as an offering, any one who practices divination, a soothsayer, or an augur, or a sorcerer, or a charmer, or a medium, or a wizard, or a necromancer (a spiritualist). For whoever does these things is an abomination to the Lord; and because of these abominable practices the Lord your God is driving them out before you.' At a séance a spirit speaking through a medium was asked, 'Do you believe in the devil?' The answer immediately came back, 'Indeed we do; he is our god and father!' That is why all forms of spiritism are expressly condemned and forbidden in Scripture.

Secondly, it is *degrading*. 'And when they say to you, "Consult the mediums and the wizards who chirp and mutter," should not a people consult their God? Should they consult the dead on behalf of the living? To the teaching and to the testimony (— the Scriptures)! Surely for this word which they speak (these mediums and wizards who chirp and mutter), there is no dawn' (—no light shed upon the truth)— (Isaiah 8.19-20). When we have God's pure and powerful Word and His supreme revelation in His Son Jesus Christ, and when we have all that we need to know about our present and our future, as well as about our guilty past, to turn to mediums and wizards is utterly degrading.

Thirdly, it is *deceptive*. Jesus warned His disciples in Matthew 24. 24., 'False Christs and false prophets will arise and show great signs and wonders, so as to lead astray, if possible, even the elect.' (cf 2 Thess. 2.9f). A woman pastor I know once told me of a couple who had begun to attend her church regularly. She asked them if they would like to consider becoming members of the church, and they replied, 'We'd like to, yes; but we are not quite sure if you would be entirely happy if we told you all about ourselves. We have to be honest: for the last five years our life has been wonderfully guided by a ouija board. It has told us about our business life, about the house which we should buy, and it even told us to come to your church.' That last point was a masterly deceptive stroke — 'it even told us to come to your church.' But they went on to say how much they had prospered since they started consulting their ouija board for everything. The wise pastor said nothing. She knew they were terribly deceived; and so she spent two days in prayer and fasting for them, praying that the spirit behind this thing would reveal itself. She went back to their house after two days. It was one of those houses which was always beautifully tidy, with everything in its place. But when she entered the front door it was as though a tornado had been through that house. The whole place was in absolute chaos and the couple were distraught beyond measure. You see, the spirit behind this thing had revealed itself to be a spirit of destruction! The devil is a murderer from the very beginning.

Fourthly, these things are *damaging*. One of the leading spiritists in America has said he did not know of a single case of spiritism where the study had been pursued without distinct deterioration of physical, mental or spiritual faculties. That is the testimony of a spiritist! It is *damaging spiritually*. Dr. Koch mentions a fascinating point in his book *Occult Bondage and Deliverance*. 'For years,' he says, 'I have witnessed the truth of this fact, that magic and almost all other occult practices either destroy the Christian faith of a person or just prevent it from developing. And yet one finds that there is no conflict between sorcery and all the other world religions.'[1] Here again is the uniqueness of the Christian faith. The other religions can naturally embrace occultism. Only Christianity finds the most tremendous clash between the powers of darkness and the powers of light — for Christianity alone is the truth.

It is *damaging mentally*. I think of one very fine mature Christian girl in our own congregation, who about a year ago came under a most suicidal depression. She says on three occasions she was right on the brink of committing suicide. She was counselled by doctors and Christian workers; and I talked to her and prayed with her. Still she was utterly depressed. She was unable to concentrate on any work and was sleeping long hours. She was brought by a friend to one of our half nights of prayer, and there the whole body

1 Op. cit., page 18.

of Christ gathered round her; and we really prayed earnestly for her, claiming the victory of the Name of Jesus. We were given a strong and lively faith in the risen and powerful Lord; and that girl was instantly and completely delivered from her depression. She then wrote a long letter to me describing all the things which she had not been able to say before, when she was depressed. What had happened was this: she comes from a broken home, and her mother in fact is an active spiritualist. Although this girl is always a bit fearful of going to see her mother and Christians had been specifically praying for her on this occasion, when she went home her mother spoke to her about occultism until the small hours of the morning, during which time she uttered two satanic prophecies in the girl's presence. Immediately this awful oppression and darkness descended on the girl, and she was utterly depressed. Occultism can be so damaging mentally.

It can also be *damaging physically*, and there are cases of paralysis and deafness and dumbness and so on, which have resulted from this. Therefore, beware of the devil and all his works. Never play with these things; and I would strongly advise you not to try to deliver a person oppressed by Satanic powers, unless you really know what you are doing. Have a healthy respect for Satan's activity, but with a confidence in the all powerful Name of Jesus. However, don't rush into things, don't play with things which could turn out to be tremendously powerful. It is like playing with a hand-grenade; you never know when it is going to go off.

Further, if you have had any personal contact with these things, repent specifically for them, and ask for cleansing and deliverance through the precious blood of Jesus. Then put on the whole armour of God, seek to stand firm, and be strong in the Lord and in the strength of His might. And it is along these lines that we turn positively and confidently in the last two chapters of this book.

# CHAPTER FOUR

# 'BATTLE ORDERS'

*'Finally, be strong in the Lord and in the strength of his might. Put on the whole armour of God, that you may be able to stand against the wiles of the devil. For we are not contending against flesh and blood, but against the principalities, against the powers, against the world rulers of this present darkness, against the spiritual hosts of wickedness in the heavenly places. Therefore take the whole armour of God, that you may be able to withstand in the evil day, and having done all, to stand. Stand therefore, having girded your loins with truth, and having put on the breastplate of righteousness, and having shod your feet with the equipment of the gospel of peace; above all taking the shield of faith, with which you can quench all the flaming darts of the evil one. And take the helmet of salvation, and the sword of the Spirit, which is the word of God. Pray at all times in the Spirit, with all prayer and supplication. To that end keep alert with all perseverence, making supplication for all the saints, and also for me, that utterance may be given me in opening my mouth boldly to proclaim the mystery of the gospel, for which I am an ambassador in chains; that I may declare it boldly, as I ought to speak' (Ephesians 6. 10-20).*

Here is the most important teaching for the active Christian soldier to be found anywhere in the entire Bible. Paul

shows both the reality of Christian warfare and the wonderful victory that God gives us in Jesus Christ.

Notice, first of all, the context of this passage. Paul's
letter to the Ephesians has been called the 'Alps of the
New Testament', because here you get the most breathtaking
view of the 'heavenly places' and of God's riches which He
has provided for us in Christ: 'Blessed be the God and Father
of our Lord Jesus Christ, who has blessed us in Christ with
every spiritual blessing in the heavenly places' (1.3). In 1.18ff
he is praying that 'the eyes of your hearts (may be) enlightened, that you may know what is the hope to which
he has called you, what are the riches of his glorious in-
heritance in the saints, and what is the immeasurable great-
ness of his power in us who believe, according to the working of his great might which he accomplished in Christ when
he raised him from the dead and made him sit at his
right hand in the heavenly places . . .' In 2.6. he rejoices
in the fact that God has 'raised us up with him, and made
us sit with him in the heavenly places in Christ Jesus.' In
3.17 he is praying again 'that Christ may dwell in your
hearts through faith; that you, being rooted and grounded
in love, may have power to comprehend with all the saints
what is the breadth and length and height and depth, and
to know the love of Christ which surpasses knowledge, that
you may be filled with all the fulness of God.' In 5.18ff he
says, 'Be filled with the Spirit, addressing one another in
psalms and hymns and spiritual songs, singing and making
melody to the Lord with all your heart, always and for
everything giving thanks in the name of our Lord Jesus
Christ to God the Father.'

When I read verses like that, I feel I have no breath left
in me! Here is a most glorious view of our wealth in Jesus
Christ — 'that you may be filled with all the fulness of
God!' *And then* comes this teaching on Christian warfare.
The fact remains that the more you long to know God and
the more you long to be the best for God and the more you

long daily to be filled with His Holy Spirit, the more you must train as a soldier of Jesus Christ because you will inevitably be plunged into this battle. The Rev. James Philip, who has written a very helpful commentary on Ephesians 6, says this: 'To be filled with the Holy Spirit is not the answer to the problems of the believer, but the signal for problems and attacks really to begin in earnest.'[1]

Praise God that they will be problems of life, rather than problems of death! But we shall only begin to know about Christian warfare when we begin to know something of the power of the Holy Spirit. In fact I believe that every Christian should have a testimony to what he has *suffered* for Christ. Many people stand up and give testimonies of blessings and experiences that they have received from Christ. However, if these are genuine blessings we shall also, before very long, have a testimony to what we have suffered for Christ. Paul was not ashamed to remind his readers that he had known what it was to suffer with Christ and to experience the fellowship of His sufferings.

## Some general facts about the Battle

*First, our own strength*: Nothing at all! Jesus said, 'without me you can do nothing.' Most of us, I think, tend to live and act as if that were a slight exaggeration. We feel that we can do some things by ourselves. Of course we need the Lord's help, especially when we are doing something rather difficult. 'No!' says Jesus, 'without me you can do nothing'—not a thing that is of value in the sight of God. Therefore, God, as I have often found in my own experience, may allow us to be knocked about in the heat of the battle until we begin to learn our *utter* weakness and helplessness without Christ. This is one of the great lessons that Paul learned when he says in 2 Corinthians 12. 7 ff that 'to keep me from being too elated by the abundance of revelations, a

*The Christian Warfare and Armour*, p. 6. (Privately Printed)

thorn was given me in the flesh, a messenger of Satan, to harass me, to keep me from being too elated. Three times I besought the Lord about this, that it should leave me; but he said to me, "My grace is sufficient for you, for my power is made perfect in weakness." I will all the more gladly boast of my weaknesses, that the power of Christ may rest upon me. For the sake of Christ, then, I am content with weaknesses, insults, hardships, persecutions and calamities; for when I am weak, then I am strong!' Our lives are like an empty glass. If you are thirsty, an empty glass cannot help you. However many convention meetings this glass may attend, however many Bible Reading it may listen to, this glass cannot help you! It will never be able to help you in your thirst. Of course, if this glass was filled with water, it would be a different matter  Water can quench your thirst, but not the glass. The New Testament says that we are no more than 'an earthen vessel'—or just an empty glass, if you like. Indeed, to our dying day, we shall never *in ourselves* be any more than an empty glass. 'Without me', says Jesus, 'you can do nothing.' Our own strength is nil.

Therefore, in Ephesians 6.10 Paul says, 'Finally, be strong in the Lord and in the strength of his might. Put on the whole armour of God.' The New English Bible translates this 'Put on all the armour which God provides'. The most vivid illustration of this in the Old Testament is in the battle between David and Goliath. David had first to reject the armour that Saul offered him, and then he took the armour which God was offering him. What was that armour? What were the weapons that God provided? David came against Goliath with this supreme confidence: 'You come to me with a sword and with a spear and with a javelin; but I come to you in the name of the Lord of hosts, the God of the armies of Israel, whom you have defied.' That was his armour, his weapon and his strength: the Name of the Lord of hosts. 'Be strong in the Lord.' So often today our strength and trust lie in strategy or publicity or organisation. and we wander into the battle forgetting the most important weapons of all. To misquote another great hymn:

> Onward Christian soldiers,
> Each to war resigned,
> With the Cross of Jesus
> Vaguely kept in mind.

No, says Paul, 'be strong in the Lord and in the power of his might.' Notice that word 'in'. We must abide in Christ, just as a plug for an electric light must be connected with the power socket; take the plug out of that socket, and there is no light. Put that plug into a text book about electric lights —there is no light! Put it into attractive leaflets put out by the Electricity Board—there is no light! There is only one place which gives power to the light. And there is only one place where you and I can be strong in this battle, and that is 'in the Lord', abiding in Him.

*Secondly, the enemy's strength:* 'We are not contending against flesh and blood, but against the principalities, against the powers . . .' The enemy is both powerful and intelligent; and unless we understand this, often we shall be defeated, depressed, harassed and ineffective. There are three main forms of attack, as seen from this passage:

1. *Subtlety:* 'Put on the whole armour of God, that you may be able to stand against the *wiles* of the devil (v. 11). In the last chapter we looked at his wiles in terms of an Angel of Light, the Father of Lies, and the Serpent. Therefore, in Ephesians 4.13ff Paul urges his readers to go on 'to mature manhood, to the measure of the stature of the fulness of Christ; so that we may no longer be children, tossed to and fro and carried about with every wind of doctrine, by the cunning of men, by their craftiness in deceitful wiles.' Never under-estimate the subtlety of the enemy. Indeed, quite a good test for Christian maturity is this: how much do you understand about the wiles of the devil? The New Testament epistles were written simply because the Christians

in those early days were so often deceived by the devil, and
Paul had to write careful, detailed instructions, saying in
effect, 'Now don't be children, tossed to and fro, but be mature, be strong; understand the wiles of the devil; don't be
knocked about by him!'

2. *Siege*: 'Therefore take the whole armour of God, that
you may be able to withstand *in the evil day*' (v. 13). This, I
believe, refers to a serious and sometimes prolonged assault
of the evil one, maybe through a time of severe illness, or an
accident which for the moment knocks you right out of the
battle; or it may be a time of continuing dark depression.

A few years ago I had a very serious illness. There were
many nights in which I could scarcely sleep at all. Frequent-
ly, during those long hours of the night, I read and re-read
the Psalms; they seemed to speak so vividly of my experience. One of my favourite Psalms at that time was Psalm
13 where the psalmist says, 'How long, O Lord? Wilt thou
forget me for ever? How long wilt thou hide thy face from
me? How long must I bear pain in my soul, and have sor-
row in my heart all the day? How long shall my enemy be
exalted over me?' How long, how long, how long? 'Consider
and answer me, O Lord my God; lighten my eyes, lest I sleep
the sleep of death.' Many Christians experience this seige
from Satan, and cry out in their hearts, 'How long, O Lord?
How long, how long?'

James Philip wrote at the beginning of his commentary on
Christian Warfare, 'The teaching of this passage became very
real and came to mean a great deal to me when I was passing through a time of fierce and prolonged testing, when all
the powers of darkness seemed to be let loose on my soul
and were intent, so it seemed, on bringing me crashing
down; and it was in these days that God revealed to me two
things: the richness and completeness of our position in
Christ and what He has made us in Him, and the divine
provision in the armour of light against all the assaults of
the enemy. In those days morning prayer for me was a mat-

ter of poring over this passage in urgent desperation, seeking to put on this divine armour piece by piece, to preserve me against the assaults of the devil that were sure to come before the day was was very far advanced'.[1]

3. *Surprise:* In verse 16 Paul talks about the *'flaming darts of the evil one'*. We shall look at these darts more carefully in a moment, but often they come just before, or just after, a time of great blessing.

However, alongside these three forms of attack there are three stages in defence.

## Our defence

1. *Strategic Retreat.* 'Be strong *in the Lord*!' This suggests that we need a shelter to hide in. Some Christians try to run away from their problems; they shut themselves up with themselves, they become moody and depressed, and perhaps they run away from Christian fellowship. The vital thing to remember is that shelter. Jean Rees once said, 'When God gives you loneliness, don't try to fill it with other things; the Lord wants you to fill it with Himself.' 'The name of the Lord is a strong tower; the righteous man runs into it and is safe.' My wife has found this lesson of great importance over the last two or three years. At times she has felt very depressed (of course when living with me this is not very surprising!), but she has learned increasingly to 'run into this strong tower of the Lord' and to close the door. There she finds that the Lord gives her wonderful strength as she rests in Him.

Let me give you another illustration of this 'strong tower'. On one University mission a young man came up after a meeting and asked if he could see me the next day, and we fixed an appointment. When the time came, he brought a girl with him; and as that girl entered the room I had the most overpowering sense of evil—a most awful, cold,

[1] op. cit. p. 1.

clammy, horrible feeling that almost knocked me over. I gripped the side of the table beside me, and in this moment of sudden fear, I 'ran away to Christ'. Quickly I claimed the power of His Name; instantly the fear left me, and I was able then to counsel them. She turned out to be a practising medium! We need at times to make a strategic retreat, to run away for a moment into Christ, and there we find our strength.

2. *Unyielding Defence.* In verses 11, 13 and 14, Paul says, 'Stand, Stand, Stand, Stand!' In other words, don't give in, don't surrender, determine at all costs that you are going to win this fight. How can you stand? Why, 'put on the whole armour of God . . . take the whole armour of God' (vv 11. 13) You cannot stand in your own strength. As the hymn puts it,

> Stand, then, in His great might,
> With all His strength endued;
> And take, to arm you for the fight,
> The panoply of God.'

3. *All-out Attack,* as you take the sword of the Spirit and rush out, as it were, to drive Satan away. We need to be positive in this battle. I asked a Christian the other day 'How are you?' He looked at me gloomily and said, 'Well, all right at the moment!' as though just waiting for something to go wrong. I have noticed in my own life how easy it is, when someone says 'How are you? Are you all right?', to reply immediately 'Oh, I had a bad night last night' (or whatever misfortune it might be). We forget about the countless blessings we have had. We tend to think about the one thing which may have been difficult. Therefore we need to be so positive.

I was once helped by a little tract called *What do you say?* by T. L. Osborn. He begins 'You said you did not have faith, and that moment, doubt arose like a giant and bound you. Perhaps you never realised that, to a great extent, you are ruled by your words. You talk failure, and failure held you in bondage. You talked fear, and fear increased its grip on you. (The answer?) We must fill our hearts with "Thus saith the Lord". Then we must confess that Word until it becomes a part of our nature.' Be very positive, holding firm the promises of God.

## The Armour

Notice a few general points. In the first place there is *no protection for the back*. Protection is given only if we face the foe and are determined to fight him. The Bible says that if any one turns back, God has no pleasure in him (Hebrews 10.38). I would say, from my own experience, that a back-slider is a most miserable and unhappy person. Sometimes a Christian plays with the world, and he feels that he is having the best of both worlds. He is in fact having the *worst* of both worlds. He has too much of the world to enjoy Christ, and too much of Christ to enjoy the world. He is in a wretched condition. There is no protection for the back.

Secondly, *the whole armour is needed*. One part protects the heart but not the head, another the head but not the heart, and so on. We need every single piece. You cannot pick and choose the pieces as you will.

Further, of the six pieces mentioned in verses 14-17, the first three should be on all the time. You can see this from the words in the text: 'Stand, therefore, *having* girded your loins with truth, and *having* put on the breastplate of right-eousness, and *having* shod your feet with the equipment of the gospel of peace'. These are on all the time. But the second three need to be taken up when the fight is on. Paul changes his expression in verse 16: '*Taking* the shield of faith . . . *Take* the helmet of salvation, and *(take)* the sword of the Spirit.' Here is the picture; a soldier is sitting in his tent and he is waiting for the battle call. He has on his belt, his breastplate and his boots; and suddenly the bugle blows.

He picks up his shield, he puts on his helmet, he grasps his sword — and he is ready for battle!

First, *The Belt of Truth*: this is vital for the rest of the armour. When I was in the Army, I remember one occasion when the R.S.M. on the parade ground suddenly turned to a new recruit and shrieked at the top of his voice, 'Jones, you are stark naked!' We all looked round to see this amazing sight on the parade ground! Jones in fact was perfectly normally and modestly dressed, but he had simply forgotten to put his belt on. In the Army this was equivalent, in the eyes of the Sergeant Major, to being stark naked, because the belt is so important.

Now the 'belt of truth' means something like this: Your whole Christian life should be held together with truth. You cannot live on feelings and experiences alone, however precious they may be to you at times. You must live on the solid, objective truth of God's Word. First, then, we must *know the truth*. That is why you find in all Paul's epistles for example, some very solid doctrine coming before the practical application. He is saying in effect, 'this is our position in Christ, now act in the light of it; become what you are.' Some Christians do not know what they are in Christ, and therefore do not know what to become or how to become it. You remember that in Romans 6 Paul kept on saying, 'Don't you know? We know! We know! You must consider.' Therefore never despise doctrine. If you have no belt of truth, you cannot possibly keep the rest of the armour in place.

Let me just illustrate the practical importance of this belt by looking at some verses from the end of Romans chapter 8. Remember that the devil is always trying to undermine our confidence in the Lord. He is the great accuser. And in Romans 8.31ff we can see this belt of truth as God's answer to four common accusations. The devil says 'You can't cope with your situation'. But in v.31 Paul replies 'What then shall we say to this? If God be for us, who is against us?' The devil comes again and says, 'You're not a real Christian; look at your life.' Paul answers in v.33 'Who shall bring any charge against God's elect? It is God who justifies.' The devil says, 'You're such a failure!' But Paul asks in v.34, 'Who is to condemn? Is it Christ Jesus, who died, yes, who was raised from the dead, who is at the right hand of God, who indeed interceded for us?' Again the devil says, 'God doesn't love you'; and in v.35ff Paul replies, 'Who shall separate us from the love of Christ? Shall tribulation or distress . . .? For I am sure that (nothing) . . . will be able to separate us from the love of God in Christ Jesus our Lord.'

There was once a young missionary going out on her first term of service to the mission field, and she was sent into a remote part of the country to live with an older missionary who had become spiritually dead and hardened in her ways. The older missionary made life, from the very first moment, impossible and intolerable for the young missionary, and this girl, within a matter of days, began to feel much resentment and bitterness that God had put her into this situation. She realised her entire missionary work was at stake. What could she do? This is what she did. She prayed for the older missionary every day, and every day she read, on her knees, 1 Corinthians 13, that great chapter on love. That, for her, was the belt of truth which she put on day by day. By the end of a whole year of praying and reading 1 Corinthians 13, she had been given such a love for this older, hardened companion, that that older woman broke down — overwhelmed by the love of this young woman. The whole situation was entirely transformed, because of that belt of truth.

Therefore, we must not only know the truth, *we must also show the truth*. There must be a most obvious sincerity and integrity about our lives. The truth of God's Word should be more manifest from our lives than from our lips. I was recently struck by some words of the Rev. Duncan Campbell: 'The greatest thing about us all is not what we say, it is not what we do; the greatest thing about us all is our unconscious influence, and that unconscious influence impregnated by the life of Jesus.'[1]

'Not merely in the words you say,
Not only in your deeds confessed,
But in the most unconscious way
Is Christ expressed.'

Some Christians live double lives: angels at church; devils at home! How many of us have some secret sin that is spoiling that unconscious influence for Jesus? It may be something that we dare not tell to any other person, something of which no-one else knows, not even the members of our own family. We have not even told Jesus and confessed it to Him; therefore there is no unconscious influence of the fragrance of Christ in our life. I believe, too, that the belt of truth suggests also a readiness for the battle. We must have the A.B.C. of the Gospel at our finger tips, ready at any moment to lead a person to Christ. If someone stopped you today and said, 'Excuse me, could you please tell me how I could find Christ?' could you today lead that person step by step to a simple faith in Christ? Do you know at least 6 verses which could help that person to find Christ? For those who are not sure, I have suggested a simple framework in the appendix on page 102.

Next we have the *Breastplate of Righteousness*. This means a life that is right with God and with man. Paul says in Acts 24. 16 'I always take pains to have a clear conscience toward God and toward men'. This is extremely important, because if my life is not right with God and with man, I have no 'breastplate', and I am very vulnerable indeed. I meet Christians from time to time who are having severe doubts; or maybe the 'fire' has died down in their life and there is little real love for Jesus. Often this is caused by some

[1] *The Price and Power of Revival*, p. 31. (The Faith Mission).

sin and disobedience. There needs to be repentance somewhere. Maybe there is bitterness or resentment towards another person. Something has soured their life and spoilt their
relationship with Jesus; and there is no breastplate. I remember once having on my back a huge boil, and I was very
depressed. I had lots of kind Christian friends who were
full of sympathy: 'How Satan is attacking you! You are
right in the front line, of course, and a special target for
Satan's attack.' It was flattering but I knew what God was
saying to my heart and conscience. There was unconfessed
sin in my life. I was disobedient. I had no breastplate of
righteousness, and God was using that unpleasant experience
with the boil to trouble my own conscience until at last
I had to confess that sin and get right with God. Please
don't conclude from that that every time you get a boil
there is something wrong in your life! However, when we
have some unpleasant experience we ought to ask the question, 'Lord, what are you saying to me in this?' You see,
faith and obedience go hand in hand; and if there is disobedience, I may claim God's promises, I may plead the
Name of Jesus, I may go to prayer meetings, but it will make
no difference whatever. 'If I cherish iniquity in my heart
the Lord will not hear me'. Indeed, although James gives
us the promise, 'Resist the devil and he will flee from you',
he begins by saying 'Submit yourselves therefore to God.
Resist the devil and he will flee from you. Draw near to
God and he will draw near to you. Cleanse your hands, you
sinners, and purify your hearts, you men of double mind'
(James 4. 7-8). It is only as our life is right with God that
we can resist the devil with any obvious results. Because,
when our life is right with God, He gives us the perfect
righteousness of Christ — our glorious breastplate.

Next we have the *Boots of the Gospel*: 'Having shod your
feet with the equipment of the gospel of peace.' The Roman
soldier wore heavy sandals, equivalent to the army boots
of today. In part this means obviously a readiness and
eagerness to preach the gospel: 'How beautiful are the feet

of those who preach good news.' When I was in the Army,
the first thing I did after some strenuous exercise was to
take off those heavy boots and put on some slippers instead.
However there are far too many Christians today who belong
to the 'carpet-slipper brigade', who prefer to stay at home
by the fireside and watch their favourite television pro-
gramme. Of course they might be willing to share their
testimony of Christ if someone happened to call. But they
are not willing to put on their boots and to go out into
enemy territory. The early Christians kept their gospel boots
on all the time. It was tough going; they were persecuted;
many of them shed blood. But if they had taken off those
gospel boots the church would have died in the first century, and you and I would not have been Christians today.
If the Communists had taken their boots off in 1917, the
Revolution would have got no further than Moscow. But
they have kept their boots on, and now one-third of the
world is in communist hands.

Moreover, the Roman soldier needed these boots for two
main purposes. First, they gave him *firmness*, stopping him
from slipping and sliding all over the place; and that quality
is so vital in Christian warfare — 'to stand firm'. There are
too many 'nice' Christians, who will say and do what other
people want them to say and do: men-pleasers, yes-men.
There is no firmness; and with the pressure of the world
and the influence of false teaching some Christians today
slip and slide all over the place. 'Stand firm!' says Paul.
Put on those boots.

Secondly, the boots refer to *mobility*. They enabled a
soldier to move quickly and easily over rough, unfamiliar
ground. And I believe that we Christians need to learn a
great deal about being mobile in a rapidly changing situation in society. Not that the Gospel should change, certainly
not! That is always the same. But our presentation and our
approach must change. One lesson I am having to learn all
the time, particularly in student evangelism, is that you can-

not go on using old methods which were designed for a completely different generation.

Next we come to the *Shield of Faith*: 'Above all taking the shield of faith, with which you can quench all the flaming darts of the evil one.' These flaming darts were flame-tipped arrows, and there was usually a barrage of these before the main assault — the 'artillery' firing before the infantry went in. Therefore these flaming darts represent fierce, sudden and unexpected attacks. What are your first waking thoughts each morning? Be honest! What do you think about first thing on Monday morning when the alarm goes off? Be honest! I know what my first thoughts are like when I am tired and have a very busy day ahead; but I am learning to take up the shield of faith: 'Thank you Lord for this new day. Praise the Lord! Wonderful Lord Jesus!' Sometimes I lie in bed for a few moments quietly rejoicing in the Lord; I know only too well how these first waking thoughts can be so negative. A friend of mine was host to a travelling evangelist, and when he brought him an early morning cup of tea he tiptoed quietly across the bedroom where the man was sleeping. Suddenly the evangelist sat bolt upright in bed, threw his arms in the air, and said 'Praise the Lord!' My friend almost dropped the tea-pot! Over breakfast he said, 'Forgive this personal question, but do you always sit bolt upright in bed and say "Praise the Lord!" like that?' He replied, 'Yes, I learned that so often the devil attacks my mind and imagination before I have even got out of bed, so I now take up the shield of faith first thing.' (My advice is that you have a quiet word with your wife or your husband before you do that tomorrow!)

Again, you may find sudden and unexpected evil thoughts when praying or when studying your Bible; or perhaps sudden fierce doubts. Perhaps you have known sudden panic or fear or lust, and you are taken by complete surprise. Maybe you experience unexpected persecution, or illness, or waves of depression. Or perhaps you have been praying for

guidance, and you have sharp attacks of doubt afterwards.
Well, recognise the attacks of the enemy — those fiery
darts — and lift up the shield of faith.

One delightful illustration of all this, in spite of its quaint-
ness, is the story of Billy Bray. Billy Bray was a miner in
Cornwall during the nineteenth century, and remarkably
used by God. Here he described how he resisted the devil
with the shield of faith. ' "The devil knows where I live" was
a common saying of Billy's, in answer to persons who said
that he knew but little of trial and temptation. He was
tempted, so he said, to do many bad things . . . and sometimes to end his life by throwing himself down the "shaft"
of a mine!!' Notice that: he was a fine Christian worker, but
at times he was so depressed, that he was tempted to com-
mit suicide. 'But he told the tempter, "*old smutty-face*", to
do this himself, and see how he would like it!' Later in the
book he gives another account of the devil's fiery attack,
"Friends, last week I was a-diggin' up my 'taturs. It was a
wisht poor yield, sure 'nough; there was hardly a sound
one in the whole lot. An' while I was a-diggin' the devil
come to me, and he says, "Billy, do you think your Father
do love you?" "I should reckon He do," I says. "Well, I
don't," says the ould tempter in a minute. If I'd thought
about it I shouldn't ha' listened to 'en, for his 'pinions ben't
worth the leastest bit o' notice. "I don't," says he, "and I
tell 'ee what for: if your Father loved you, Billy Bray, He'd
give you a pretty yield o' 'taturs". "Pray, sir," says I,
"who may you happen to be, comin' to me a-talkin' like
this here?" ' And Billy went on to say that when he served
the devil he got some pretty miserable service, and that now
with Jesus Christ 'He's given me a clean heart, an' a soul
full o' joy, an' a lovely suit o' white as'll never wear out;
and He says that He'll make a king o'me before He've done,
and that He'll take me to His palace to reign with Him for
ever and ever. An' now you come up here a-talkin' like
that." Bless 'e, my dear friends, he went off in a minute,

like as if he'd been shot — *I do wish he had* — *and he never had the manners to say Good morning.*'[1]

Remember some of the tremendous truths about Jesus Christ. Don't give the devil any encouragement; just lift up the shield of faith.

Then we have *The Helmet of Salvation*. This is to protect the mind and our whole attitude towards the Christian faith. If Satan cannot succeed in other ways he will try to make you tired, weary, discouraged, and disillusioned. You will find in the Psalms again and again questions like this, '*Why do the wicked prosper and the righteous suffer?*' What is the answer to that? Take up the helmet of salvation! Paul declares in Romans 8.18, 'I consider that the sufferings of this present time are not worth comparing with the glory that is to be revealed to us'. He looks ahead to the future glorious salvation when at last we shall see Jesus face to face, and then all the sufferings of the present world will be lost in that first moment's welcome in heaven. That is the helmet of salvation.

Next the *Sword of the Spirit*, the only offensive weapon. What is the difference between this and the belt of truth? The belt of truth, I believe, refers to the basic essentials — the A.B.C. of the gospel. The sword of the Spirit refers to the detailed knowledge of this book, so that we know how to use it, both for ourselves and for other people. In particular notice the combination of the Word and Spirit: 'Take the sword of the Spirit which is the word of God' (v.17). The devil does not mind us taking the one without the other: the Word without the Spirit is lifeless, and the spirit without the Word could be dangerous — not the Holy Spirit of course (He is never dangerous), but isolated 'spiritual experiences'.

This leads us to the final point about the Christian's armour. As the hymn puts it, 'Put on the gospel armour.

[1] *The King's Son* by F. W. Bourne (Bible Christian Book-Room, 1877) pp. 104. 115-117.

Each piece put on with prayer'. Therefore Paul in v.18 says, 'Pray at all times in the Spirit, with all prayer and supplication.' The armour by itself is not magical. Every piece is in place. But can it fight a battle? Not at all! It needs a powerful, living person inside it before it can fight any battle. Therefore, even with all God's armour in its place we still need an utter dependence upon God. We still need the power of the Holy Spirit within us before we can fight this battle and win it for the glory of Jesus Christ. We have got to be strong *in the Lord*. Some people are strong on doctrines, but doctrines by themselves will not help us; some Christians are strong on verses, but verses by themselves will not help us. It is only the Lord who can give us the victory. 'The battle is mine and the victory is mine and the power is mine'. 'Without me you can do *nothing*!'

'Be strong in the Lord and in the strength of His might.'

# CHAPTER FIVE

# 'LIFE FOR THE WORLD'

*'For though we live in the world we are not carrying on a worldly war, for the weapons of our warfare are not worldly but have divine power to destroy strongholds'* (2 Corinthians 10. 3-4).

That would be a wonderful text to put up somewhere in our rooms, to remind us constantly of the battle that we are fighting. 'For though we live in the world we are not carrying on a worldly war'. And I cannot overstress the importance of this, because from the pattern of a great deal of Christian activity you might have thought that we *were* engaged in a worldly war. We have a problem; so at once we set up a committee. We have a task; so at once we get out plans and strategies. Someone has said, 'I was hungry, and you formed a committee to investigate my hunger. I was homeless, and you filed a report on my plight. I was sick, and you held a seminar on the situation of the under-privileged. You have investigated all aspects of my plight; but I'm still hungry, homeless and sick!' The trouble is that when we discuss things in committee (as we have to, at least to some extent), the great temptation is to think as men think and not as God thinks.

An emergency meeting of church leaders was called because of some crisis in a certain church; and the Chairman, at the start of the meeting, stood up and prayed with great fervour along these lines, 'Almighty and Eternal God,' he prayed, 'whose grace *is* sufficient for *all* things' and so on.

Immediately after his prayer he introduced the business of the meeting: 'Gentlemen,' he said, 'the situation in this Church is completely hopeless and nothing can be done!' You remember that stinging rebuke that Jesus gave to Simon Peter, when Peter meant so well and was trying so hard. Jesus has just spoken about His coming sufferings on the Cross, and Peter came out with this burst of sympathy. 'Heaven forbid! No, Lord, this shall never happen to you.' Then Jesus turned and said to Peter 'Away with you, Satan: you are a stumbling-block to me. You think as men think, not as God thinks.' (Matthew 16. 22-23, N.E.B.).

Do you see why he became a stumbling-block to Jesus? Although he was thoughtful and considerate *he was thinking as men think, not as God thinks*. That is exactly what Satan tries to make us do again and again. 'Though we live in the world we are not carrying on a worldly war, for the weapons of our warfare are not worldly but have divine power to destroy strongholds.' What are these weapons? Let me mention four, the first three very briefly.

## THE WORD OF GOD

'Take the sword of the Spirit, which is the word of God' (Ephesians 6.17). The most obvious and striking illustration of this, of course, is Jesus in the wilderness, where three times He resisted Satan by saying, 'It is written', 'It is written', 'It is written.' And those three quotations came, incidentally, from Deuteronomy chapters 6 and 8; and it is possible that Jesus had been meditating on these passages which were therefore fresh in His mind. Anyway, we must *know* the Word of God.

> 'Know it in the head,
> Stow it in the heart
> Show it in the life,
> Sow it in the world.'

I hope that, if you are following Christ, you have begun the habit of learning verses. We must know God's Word if we are going to use it.

## THE NAME OF JESUS

'At the Name of Jesus every knee must bow'. The Name of Jesus refers to His Person, to His Character, to His Authority, and to His Power. If I gave you my cheque book, and at the bottom of every blank cheque I signed my name and handed it over to you, you could have the most wonderful time (for about one week, until all the cheques began to bounce!). But if I may put it reverently like this, no cheque will bounce with God's cheque book where the promises are signed with the Name of Jesus Christ. Therefore in the Scriptures we find the Name of the Lord of crucial importance for many situations:

| | |
|---|---|
| for salvation: | Acts 4.12 |
| for protection: | Proverbs 18.10 |
| for authority: | Luke 10.17, 19 |
| for prayer: | John 14.13-14 |
| for the Holy Spirit: | John 14.26 |
| for healing: | Acts 3.6 |
| for power: | Acts 8.12 |
| for everything: | Colossians 3.17 |

Of course, this Name is not to be used as a magic formula, as the sons of Sceva soon discovered in Acts 19. 'Then some of the itinerant Jewish exorcists undertook to pronounce the name of the Lord Jesus over those who had evil spirits, saying "I adjure you by the Jesus whom Paul preaches." Seven sons of a Jewish high priest named Sceva were doing this. But the evil spirit answered them, "Jesus I know, and Paul I know; but who are you?" And the man in whom the evil spirit was leaped on them, mastered all of them, and overpowered them, so that they fled out of that house naked and wounded' (Acts 19.13-16). You can not take lightly the Name of Jesus and use it as you will. There has to be a personal relationship with Christ. There has to be a humble trust in His Name. Then, and then only, can we rightly use the power of His Name. Remember the warning, in Matthew 7, when Jesus said about the day of judgement, 'On that day many will say to me, "Lord, Lord, did we not prophesy in your name, and cast out demons in your name, and do many mighty works in your name?" And then will I declare to them, "I never knew you; depart from me, you evildoers." ' There is no magic formula in the Name of Jesus. But if you are trusting in Him as your Saviour, and if you know Him and are obeying Him, then the Name of Jesus is powerful.

## THE BLOOD OF THE LAMB

'And I heard a loud voice in heaven, saying, "Now the salvation and the power and the kingdom of our God and the authority of his Christ have come, for the accuser of our brethren has been thrown down, who accuses them day and night before our God. And they have conquered him by the blood of the Lamb and by the word of their testimony, for they loved not their lives even unto death' (Revelation 12. 10-11). I want to underline those last few words, *they loved not their lives even unto death.*' You see, even with this tremendously powerful spiritual weapon of the blood of the Lamb, there is no promise in Scripture that the warfare will not be costly. It may be very costly indeed. There is no cheap victory for anyone.

I was speaking at a missionary conference with Brother Andrew, and he told a very striking story of his last visit to Vietnam. He was travelling on a bus with a Christian in Vietnam; the bus was stationary for a moment, and a man with a basket on his back walked in front of the bus. Suddenly the Christian said, 'Watch out! In that basket there might be a bomb!' Brother Andrew asked, 'Why are you afraid?' He replied, 'Well, that man might be a Vietcong who would throw himself and the basket at the bus. He's not afraid to lose his life; but I am.' Brother Andrew made to us this comment: 'That is just the trouble with Christians today. We are not willing to lose our lives for Jesus' sake; but there are countless people in the world today who *are* willing to lose their lives for the sake of communism or for some other ideology. But how many Christians love not their lives even unto death?'

You may know this challenge from a communist: 'The gospel is a much more powerful weapon for renewal of society than is our marxist philosophy; but all the same it is *we* who will finally beat you. We communists do not play with words; we are realists, and seeing that we are determined to achieve our object we know how to obtain the means. How can anyone believe in the supreme value of your gospel if you do not practise it, if you do not spread it, if you sacrifice neither time nor money for it. We believe in our communist message, and we are ready to sacrifice everything, even our life. But you people are afraid to soil your hands.' Christ's victory cost Him His own blood.

On the Cross, of course, Christ not only dealt with our sin-problem, for which we praise God; but He also dealt with Satan himself. There, on the Cross, 'He disarmed the principalities and powers and made a public example of them, triumphing over them in him' (Colossians 2. 15). Although we are contending not against flesh and blood but against principalities and powers, on the Cross Christ has disarmed those principalities and powers. Therefore the Cross is a tremendous triumph. Satan hates the preaching of the Cross of Christ. No wonder! Because through death Christ has destroyed 'him who has the power of death, that is, the devil, and (has delivered) all those who through fear of death were subject to lifelong bondage' (Hebrews 2. 14). Further, one verse in particular has often given me encouragement when it comes to this battle. John in his first letter tells us that 'the Son of God appeared to destroy the works of the devil'. In the Greek this really means that He came to 'untie', to 'undo' the works of the devil. The devil tries to tie us up in knots, hundreds of them; and Christ comes to untie all those knots and set His people free. What a beautiful picture of Christ unravelling those knots! My little girl, aged 5, sometimes comes to me with a most terrible mess of string or wool. 'Daddy, can you untie it?' And Daddy has to sit down for half an hour to unravel this mess! Christ comes to untie all those knots of the devil; and it is wonderful to remember that 'greater is He that is within you than he that is in the world'. Never be afraid.

## THE POWER OF THE HOLY SPIRIT

Even after Christ's resurrection the disciples were still, for at least six weeks, timid, frightened, and uncertain as to how they were ever going to carry out their commission to be witnesses to Jesus. They knew the Word of God, they believed in the Name of Jesus, they trusted in the Blood of the Lamb, but still they had none of the power and authority that they so desperately needed—until the Holy Spirit came upon them. Often I meet with Christians who have given their all to Jesus, but who have not received all that Jesus would give them.

'The grand thing the Church wants in this time is God's Holy Spirit You all get up plans and say, "Now if the Church were altered a little bit it would do better." You think if there were different ministers or different church order, or something different, then all would be well. No, dear friends, it's not there the mistake lies. It's that we want more of the Spirit. Now people are saying, "This must be altered and that must be altered", but it would go no better unless God the Spirit should come to bless us. You may have the same ministers and they should be a thousand times more useful for God if God is pleased to bless them. This is the Church's great want. And until that want be supplied, we may reform and reform and still be just the same. All we

want is the Spirit of God.' Words that might have been
written for the 1970's—but in fact spoken by Charles Spurgeon on the 31st August 1857! Billy Graham has put it like
this, 'The time has come to give the Holy Spirit His rightful
place. We need to be baptized with the Holy Spirit, we need
to know what Paul meant when he said "Be filled with the
Spirit". Give it any terminology you like, we need to accept
it, to get something, for we do not have the same dynamic
that the early Church had.' Don't get 'hung up' on terminology: whatever we call it, we need it. Therefore I want to
ask two questions: What does it mean to be filled with the
Spirit? And, How can I be filled with the Spirit?

## What does it mean to be filled with the Spirit?

Often there is some confusion on this point. What are you
looking for if you are seeking to be filled with the Spirit? Is
it a certain type of experience, something you have read
about or heard about? Several years ago, for a period of
three or four months, I was in some distress and agony,
longing to know the power of the Holy Spirit and to be more
effective in my ministry. I read stories of revival, how the
Spirit would come down and a person would be thrown to
the ground by the power of the Spirit, or suddenly in the
middle of the night he would leap out of bed and shout
'Hallelujah!' for four hours. Well, I was waiting for something to happen, but I never lept out of bed at 2 o'clock in
the morning! Not that we should be frightened of experiences,
if they are based on God's Word. You cannot possibly read
the Acts of the Apostles without seeing that they had a great
*experience* of the love of Jesus, and of the power of the
Holy Spirit. However, the devil can tie us into knots by
making us go on seeking and searching for a certain type of
experience that we have heard about or read about.

What, then, does it mean to be filled with the Spirit? In
Ephesians 5. 18 Paul gives a clear command, 'Be filled with

the Spirit.' This is not an optional extra; it is a command, God's command. But first, let me put this verse firmly into its context, to show that it is not just a 'blessed experience'. It involves at least seven things. First it involves *Walking in love:* 'Therefore be imitators of God, as beloved children. And walk in love, as Christ loved us and gave himself up for us, a fragrant offering and sacrifice to God' (Ephesians 5. 1-2). He says, 'imitators of God', because if we really are filled with the Spirit we should have something of the divine image about us, especially this quality of love; God *is* love. It is interesting to notice that where, in the Acts of the Apostles, Luke says about four or five times 'the Holy Spirit fell' on a group of people, that word 'fell' is used in four or five other times in the New Testament in the context of an 'affectionate embrace'. We cannot build a doctrine on this, but it suggests that when the Holy Spirit 'falls' on people, God gives them an 'affectionate embrace', or rather, they are overwhelmed with the love of God. That, I believe, was the essence of the power at Pentecost: they were so overwhelmed with divine love, that later Paul could say 'the love of Christ controls us'. And because they loved Him with all their heart, and because His love was constantly filling their lives, they went on and on. People hated them, opposed them, persecuted them. But nothing could stop them, because of this overpowering love. Love is the hallmark of the Holy Spirit. And if anyone claims some blessing of the Spirit I normally look for two things: first, is Christ glorified, because the Holy Spirit always comes to glorify Christ. And, secondly, is there love, because if there is no love, whatever else we may have, we have nothing at all. In 1 Corinthians chapter 13, Paul talks about tongues, prophecy, spiritual understanding, faith, generosity, self-sacrifice—all excellent things—but, without love, *nothing*! And if we are to show signs of being filled with the Spirit, we must be walking in love.

Second, *Walking in the Light*. 'For once you were darkness, but now you are light in the Lord; walk as children of light'

(5.8). In other words, be in constant and perfect fellowship with God—constant and perfect, not because *we* are perfect, but because the blood of Jesus goes on and on cleansing us from sin. As the tear water in the eye goes on cleansing the eye, so the blood of Jesus goes on cleansing us from sin. Of course, there must be a conscious, deliberate and complete break with all known sin. 'But immorality and all impurity or covetousness must not even be named among you, as is fitting among saints. Let there be no filthiness, nor silly talk nor levity, which are not fitting; but instead let there be thanksgiving' (5.3f).

The Holy Spirit is the *Holy* Spirit, and God will not fill a vessel if it is unclean. If my wife asks me for a drink of water, I might go into the kitchen and pick up a glass. However, if it is not very clean, I do one of two things: either I wash it there and then, or else I put it on one side and take another glass instead. In the same way, if God is going to fill a person with His Holy Spirit, either He must first cleanse that person from all his sin (depending on that person's repentance), or He will put that person on one side for the moment, and take someone else for the task that He has. The Holy Spirit is the *Holy* Spirit. There is no substitute for obedience. Paul underlines this fact again and again in Ephesians 5.

Third, *Praise and Thanksgiving*. 'Do not get drunk with wine, for that is debauchery; but be filled with the Spirit, addressing one another in psalms and hymns and spiritual songs, singing and making melody to the Lord with all your heart, always and for everything giving thanks in the name of our Lord Jesus Christ to God the Father' (5.18-20). What a wonderful picture that is! Joyful singing, of course, is always linked with times of spiritual revival. It is the expression of someone who is so full of the Spirit that he longs to worship and praise and adore. At Pentecost they said 'We hear them telling in our own tongues the mighty works of God.' The 120 were full of praise! We should not be frightened' of such an experience of the love of God that we ourselves are lost in wonder, love and praise. In most churches we are so frightened of emotion. I am an Anglican clergyman, and the Bishop of Coventry once said, 'Delirious emotionalism is not the chief peril of the English clergy!' Many of us are so staid and formal and correct—and dull! At Pentecost the crowd thought the disciples were drunk because of this wonderful 'wine' of the Holy Spirit. Dr. Tozer once said that if Christians are forbidden to enjoy the wine of the Spirit they will turn instead to the wine of the flesh. 'Our teachers took away our right to be happy in God, and the human heart has wreaked its terrible vengeance by going on a fleshly binge from which the evangelical church will not soon recover, if indeed it ever does. Christ died for our hearts, and the Holy Spirit wants to come and satisfy them.'[1] And the heart that is full of the Holy Spirit will want to sing for joy. Moreover, praise is honouring to God and strengthening for ourselves: 'the joy of the Lord is your strength'.

Fourth, *Right Relationships:* 'Be subject to one another out of reverence for Christ' (v. 21), and at once Paul goes on to speak of love and humility within Christian fellowship. Instead of pride, suspicion, jealousy, or criticism, the love of Christ should so permeate our lives and fellowship that others will say 'See how they love one another.' Then Paul goes on immediately to speak of husbands and wives: 'Wives, be subject to your husbands, as to the Lord ... Husbands, love your wives, as Christ loved the Church', and so on. I would say that in a Christian couple the marriage relationship between them is the most important thing after their relationship to the Lord Himself. In 1 Peter we are told that husbands and wives must watch this relationship or else our prayers will be hindered. However, other relationships too are important, and Paul goes on to write about parent and child, and master and servant.

[1] *The Root of the Righteous.* (Send the Light Trust).

Now, I think it is very significant that this question of relationships comes *immediately* after the command to be filled with the Spirit. A student missionary council did some survey into the causes of first term failures from the mission field. From a hundred missionaries who had come home they found the main causes were these.

Insufficient devotional life—9%

Failure to accept discipline—16%

Inability to work with others—17%

Feeling of superiority over natives—17%

Friction between husband and wife—9%

Lack of personal discipline—11%

Other forms of laziness—17%

Problems of sex—4%

Most of those things indicate something wrong in terms of personal relationships.

Briefly, there are three other matters that Paul talks about in the context of 'being filled with the Spirit': *Spiritual Warfare* (we have looked at that in some detail in the previous chapteer); much *Prayer* (6.18 'Pray at all times in the Spirit, with all prayer and supplication'); and *Boldness in Witness:* Paul asks them to pray 'for me, that utterance may be given me in opening my mouth boldly to proclaim the mystery of the gospel, for which I am an ambassador in chains; that I may declare it boldly, as I ought to speak.' You will find this word 'boldness' and its associates coming again and again in the early chapters of Acts. 'They were all filled with the Holy Spirit and said "What a wonderful time we have had" '? Not a bit of it! 'They were all filled with the Holy Spirit and spoke the word of God with boldness.' The Spirit comes that Jesus may be glorified; the Spirit comes that we may be witnesses to Jesus. He does not come just for personal excitement.

### How, then, can I be filled with the Spirit?

Michael Griffiths says in his book, *Three men filled with the Spirit*, 'Our Lord taught (John 7. 37-39) that the Spirit, when He is given, will well up in us like a bubbling spring to everlasting life (cf. John 4.14.). Scripture also teaches that God has "flooded your hearts through His Spirit which is given to us" (Rom. 5. 5). If, therefore, we think of a fountain which is overflowing in such a way that it is constantly immersed you have a better notion of what "the baptism of the Spirit" ought to mean. It is not merely a past experience but rather an ever-fresh experience of constant total immersion'[1] I love that: *'an ever-fresh experience of constant total immersion'*.

Let us look at some extremely important verses on this—John 7. 37-39: 'On the last day of the feast, the great day, Jesus stood up and proclaimed, "If any one thirst, let him come to me and drink. He who believes in me, as the scripture has said, 'Out of his heart shall flow rivers of living water.' " Now this He said about the Spirit, which those who believed in Him were to receive; for as yet the Spirit had not yet been given, because Jesus was not yet glorified.' I want to pick out from these verses four verbs, Thirst, Come, Drink and Believe.

1. *Thirst.* 'If any one thirst'—this is a selective invitation. It is not to everyone just like that. But if you are thirsty to know the power of God in your life and to be an effective witness to Jesus; if you are thirsty for the fulness of the Holy Spirit; if you are thirsty to be the very best for God; *then* this invitation applies to you. And if you are *not* thirsty I would say there is something seriously wrong. When I have been away on a mission I often bring home a little present for my son and daughter (aged 2 and 5). If I say to them 'There's a little present in my study for you both', they go rushing in there as fast as they can! There would be

[1] op. cit., 34ff. (Overseas Missionary Fellowship).

something seriously wrong with them if they didn't want something that I had brought them, because they know I love them. And there is something seriously wrong if we don't want a good and wonderful gift that God has for us—because He loves us. Therefore, if we feel, to be quite honest in our own heart, that there is not very much 'thirst' at the moment, what is wrong?

Is it *ignorance* about the work of the Spirit. Or is it *fear*: fear of God, perhaps, 'What will God do with my life?' Many Christians know little of the power of the Spirit in their lives because they are still standing in the shallow end; they are afraid to get out of their depth. But it is only when God puts us into the deep end, where we really have to start 'swimming', that we may begin to cry out to Him, 'Lord, I cannot do it! I haven't the strength to do it! I desperately need your help!' But some Christians are afraid of the 'deep end'. Or perhaps we are afraid of man—what others might think or say. 'The fear of man brings a snare.'

Or is it *pride* hindering our thirst? I think I am all right as I am; I don't need any blessing. One fine missionary to India in a former generation was a man who became known as Praying Hyde. As he left England for the first time on a ship bound for India, it was a great moment for him. There he was, being sent out by the Lord; he had given everything to Jesus Christ, He was going out to the country to which God had sent him. And as the ship began to sail, he opened a letter which a minister friend had given him just before he got on board. The letter said this, 'Dear John, I shall not cease praying for you until you are filled with the Holy Spirit.' John Hyde said this, 'My pride was touched! I felt exceedingly angry, crushed the letter, threw it into the corner of the cabin, and went up on deck in a very angry spirit. The idea of him implying that I was *not* filled with the Spirit!' Then he began to reflect for a moment, and he realized that it was not honouring to God to think and feel like that. He went back to his cabin, and on his knees he searched for the letter that he had thrown aside. He found it, unravelled the crumpled mess, and read it again and again. He said, 'I felt annoyed; but the conviction was gaining on me that my friend was right and I was wrong. At last in despair I asked the Lord to fill me with the Spirit. And the moment I did this, the whole atmosphere was cleared up.'

Of course there are many other things that could spoil our thirst for God: sin, resentment, a critical spirit, a wrong relationship. John comments that 'the Spirit had not been given, because Jesus was not yet glorified'. Although there is an obvious historical reference to that, there is also a spiritual significance in that remark. If Jesus is not glorified in some part of our life, the Spirit will not be given in all His fulness.

2. *Come*. 'If any one thirst, let him come to me', says Jesus. Some people make a wrong distinction between Jesus and the Spirit. But the fact is that if we want to be filled with the Spirit we come to Jesus; and when we are filled with the Spirit, the Spirit makes Jesus more real. There is no awkward distinction, there is no conflict between the Spirit and Jesus at all. Of course not! As we come to Jesus for salvation, so we come to Him for the power of the Spirit.

3. *Drink*. This is where some people are confused. They go on asking and asking but never seem to receive. I went on for three to four months praying and praying to be filled with the Spirit, waiting for *something* to happen—but nothing happened; so I said 'Oh well, it hasn't happened this time so I'll go away and come back tomorrow!' And I went on asking to be filled with the Spirit and nothing seemed to happen. But says Jesus, 'if any one thirst let him come to me and *drink*'.

Supposing you came to my house one day and said, 'I'm rather thirsty, could you give me a drink of water?'. I would say, 'Of course!' And I would get a glass of water and fill it up for you. 'Here you are, this will quench your thirst!' and I would hand it to you and you would take it. Then I might have to leave you for ten minutes; but supposing when I came back you were still complaining of thirst because, although the glass was in your hands, you had not drunk any water! I would say, 'Well, look! There it is in your hands. Now drink!' That is ridiculous, of course. You would drink immediately if you were thirsty. Yet many people stop short at this very point with the gift of the Holy Spirit. Paul tells us that God 'has blessed us in Christ with every spiritual blessing in the heavenly places.' We have everything in Christ. Therefore, Jesus says, 'Now, drink! Receive!' It is so simple. Therefore we must look at this last word carefully.

4. *Believe.* Jesus said, 'He who believes in me, as the scripture has said, "Out of his heart shall flow rivers of living water" '. The whole essence of faith is this, that if you have a promise of God and you claim it, you must not only believe that it will be true but you must start praising God that it *is* true. Take the illustration of the Christmas story. When the angel promises to Mary the gift of a Son, what does she do? She starts praising God that it is already true. She says in that tremendous song of praise, '*The Lord has done great things for me.*' If we had been there we might have said, 'Mary, how do you know?' 'Well, He's promised.' 'Yes, but how do you *know*. You have no evidence at all apart from the truth of His promise; so how do you know?' 'Well, He's promised!' You see, she starts praising God the moment she receives His promise to her. She had to wait for the actual fulfilment of the promise in her life but she starts at once praising God that it is already true. And as she goes on praising, of course it becomes true, wonderfully true.

I have already described how I had asked to be filled with the Spirit; and I asked again and again. I had the glass there in my hand, but I was not drinking and not believing. Eventually God opened my eyes and gave me the gift of faith to believe the promise I had known so well—the promise of Jesus in Luke 11.13: 'How much more will the heavenly Father give the Holy Spirit to those who ask him!' I said, 'Lord, I believe now; and I believe that I shall receive now and I will start praising you that you have now met my need, you have filled me now with your Holy Spirit'. And as I started to praise Him I had a most wonderful, quiet sense of joy and peace in the Lord. The precise nature of the experience is not important: it differs with different people. But we need to trust that as we come to Jesus and ask for this fulness of the Spirit to witness to Him more faithfully, that He means what He promises.

Of course we must go on and on being filled with the Spirit. It is not a once-for-all blessing. We have to go on day by day. When Paul says, 'Be filled with the Spirit', the tense of the verb means 'go on and on and on being filled with the Spirit'. And as we *go on* believing in this glorious promise of Jesus, so from our heart will *go on* flowing those rivers of living water—providing our life is right with the Lord. Certainly we may sin and grieve the Spirit. But there is, praise God, the precious blood of Jesus to cleanse us again and the clear promise of Jesus to fill us again; and we can go out—feeling still weak, maybe, because in ourselves we are only empty vessels, but knowing that from our hearts, according to His promise, there will flow that living water, reaching out to the thirsty all around. Are you filled with the Spirit? Are you thirsty? Will you then come to Jesus? Will you drink? And will you believe?

**For Further Reading**

Watchman Nee:        *Love not the World*
                     (Victory Press, 1968)

Watchman Nee:        *The Normal Christian Life*
                     (Victory Press, 1957)

C. S. Lewis:         *The Screwtape Letters*
                     (Geoffrey Bles, 1942)

Michael Harper:      *Spiritual Warfare*
                     (Hodder & Stoughton, 1970)

Robert Peterson:     *Roaring Lion*
                     (O.M.F., 1968)

J. Stafford Wright:  *Christianity and the Occult*
                     (Scripture Union, 1971)

A. Skevington Wood:  *Signs of the Times*
                     (Oliphants, 1970)

Basilea Schlink:     *Ruled by the Spirit*
                     (Lakeland, 1969)

A. W. Tozer:         *Paths to Power*
                     (Oliphants, 1964)

A. W. Tozer:         *The Divine Conquest*
                     (Oliphants, 1964)

A. N. Triton:        *Whose World ?*
                     (I.V.F., 1970)

**Some verses to help someone to find Christ:**

A) Something to Admit:    The fact of sin
        Romans 3.23 and 6.23
        Isaiah 59.2

B) Something to Believe:    That Christ has died for you
        Isaiah 53.5-6
        1 Peter 3.18

C) Something to Consider:    That Christ must come first
        Mark 8.34-38

D) Something to Do:    Ask Christ into your life
        John 1.12
        Revelation 3.20

## APPENDIX C

**Victory verses for God's freedom fighters**

I John 4.4          He who is in you (God) is greater than
                    he who is in the world (Satan)

I John 3.8          The reason the Son of God appeared
                    was to destroy the works of the devil.

I John 5.4          Whatever is born of God overcomes the
                    world; and this is the victory that over-
                    comes the world, our faith.

James 4.7           Submit yourselves to God. Resist the
                    devil and he will flee from you.

Romans 6.11         Consider yourselves dead to sin and
                    alive to God in Christ Jesus.

Luke 10.19    I have given you authority to tread upon serpents and scorpions, and over all the power of the enemy; and nothing shall hurt you.

Ephesians 6.11    Put on the whole armour of God, that you may be able to stand against the wiles of the devil.

Colossians 2.15    He disarmed the principalities and powers and made a public example of them, triumphing over them in (the cross)

2 Corinthians 10.4    The weapons of our warfare are not worldly but have divine power to destroy strongholds.

Revelation 12.11    They have conquered (Satan) by the blood of the Lamb and by the word of their testimony.

Hebrews 2.14-15    That through death he might destroy him who has the power of death, that is, the devil, and deliver all those . . . subject to lifelong bondage.

I Peter 5.8-9    Your adversary the devil prowls around . . Resist him, firm in your faith.

Romans 8.31    If God is for us, who is against us?

Romans 8.37    We are more than conquerors through him who loved us.

I Corinthians 15.57    Thanks be to God, who gives us the victory through our Lord Jesus Christ.